Handbook of Digital and Multimedia Forensic Evidence

HANDBOOK
OF DIGITAL
AND
MULTIMEDIA FORENSIC
EVIDENCE

Edited by

John J. Barbara

HUMANA PRESS ✳ TOTOWA, NEW JERSEY

© 2008 Humana Press Inc.
999 Riverview Drive, Suite 208
Totowa, New Jersey 07512

www.humanapress.com

This publication is printed on acid-free paper. ∞
ANSI Z39.48-1984 (American Standards Institute)

Permanence of Paper for Printed Library Materials

Cover design by Karen Schulz
Production Editor: Michele Seugling

For additional copies, pricing for bulk purchases, and/or information about other Humana titles, contact Humana at the above address or at any of the following numbers: Tel.: 973-256-1699; Fax: 973-256-8341; E-mail: orders@humanapr.com; or visit our Website: www.humanapress.com

Printed in the United States of America. 10 9 8 7 6 5 4 3 2 1

e-ISBN 978-1-60327-124-0

Library of Congress Control Number: 2007931072.

About the Editor

Mr. Barbara has worked in forensic crime laboratories for over 30 years and currently supervises the Digital Evidence Section (Computer Forensics) in a state crime laboratory in the United States. Mr. Barbara became an American Society of Crime Laboratory Directors/Laboratory Accreditation Board (ASCLD/LAB) Legacy Inspector in 1993 and an ASCLD/LAB ISO 17025 certified Technical Assessor in 2004. He has participated in over 25 laboratory inspections for ASCLD/LAB, serving as an Inspector, Site Leader, Team Captain, and Technical Assessor. He has inspected the disciplines of Controlled Substances, Toxicology, Firearms and Toolmarks, Trace Evidence, Questioned Documents, and Digital & Multimedia Evidence (Computer Forensics, Forensic Audio, Image Analysis, and Video Analysis). On three occasions, he has assisted ASCLD/LAB with the training of their Digital & Multimedia Evidence Inspectors and was appointed by the ASCLD/LAB Board as Chairperson of its Digital & Multimedia Evidence Proficiency Review Committee. He is a member of the Editorial Advisory Board of *Forensic Magazine* and author of a regular column in *Forensic Magazine* titled "The Digital Insider." He has presented numerous information programs and workshops and has authored many articles pertaining to Digital & Multimedia Evidence Accreditation.

To Ralph M. "Bud" Keaton for your years of dedicated, uncompromising efforts to improve the quality of forensic laboratory services provided to the criminal justice system. You were there at the "dawn" of forensic laboratory accreditation, long before many of us even understood what accreditation meant. Over the years, you have been, and continue to be, a constant force promoting the necessity for forensic laboratories to become accredited. You have ensured that the accreditation process is impartial, objective, and conducted under the highest standards of ethical practice. Under your guidance, the Digital & Multimedia Evidence discipline was added to the ASCLD/LAB accreditation programs. Forensic laboratories that achieve ASCLD/LAB Legacy or ASCLD/LAB-International accreditation in this discipline (and any of the others that are offered) can be considered as having attained accreditation from the premier forensic laboratory accreditation program in the world today. Job well done "Bud!"

Preface

In April 2005, I received a telephone call from Humana Press Senior Editor, Harvey Kane, inquiring whether there might be a need for a book to be published concerning the different aspects of computer forensics. During a subsequent meeting to discuss the current state of available texts covering this topic, I noted to Mr. Kane that there were several excellent computer forensics books already published and readily available. Mr. Kane then inquired as to what were some of the commonalities and differences between those books. My response was that they all discussed computer forensics analysis in detail. (Indeed, the purpose of one in particular was to guide the individual to becoming a skilled computer forensics examiner.) Furthermore, I indicated that some of the books included topics such as different operating systems as well as chapters on evidence collection and processing. Still others dealt specifically with incident response. Mr. Kane then asked me two questions: "If a person wanted to pursue a career in computer forensics, is there any one book currently available that provides an overview?" and if not, "If you were to write a book on computer forensics, what topics would you include in the book?" The meeting ended with Mr. Kane asking me to draft a scope document concerning a possible book on computer forensics.

Shortly thereafter, I attended a local Infragard meeting. The speaker's topic for the meeting was incident response and the role that computer forensics can play in identifying the evidence of a Denial of Service (DoS) attack. After the presentation, a number of those present asked the speaker such questions as: "What training is necessary to become an examiner in this field?" "How and where can you obtain such training?" "Where can you get the software to investigate this type of crime?" "Does an information technology (IT) person have to be certified?" "How do I go about obtaining certification?" "What certifications are available?" "What are the legal issues involved in searching and seizing digital data?" "What education is necessary to be hired in the IT field?" "What happens if you have to testify in court?"

Over the past several years, I have been asked many of those same questions by high school and college students and other individuals interested in entering the computer forensics field. One question in particular stands out: "How and where does a person look to obtain the necessary information if he or she is thinking of a career in this field?" All of these questions exemplify how difficult it is at times to obtain necessary information to make career choices.

As I began to develop an outline and scope document, I reflected back upon the field as a whole, trying to determine how we got to where we are now. In doing so,

I began to identify some issues that should potentially be addressed. All of us are aware that digital and multimedia data is found everywhere in our society. From the shoplifter who is captured on video tape to the victim of identity theft, digital and multimedia data is somehow involved in the analysis of the evidence. Over the past 10 years or so, considerable emphasis has been placed on the need to find, capture, store, examine, and preserve digital and multimedia data for investigative purposes. There are many practitioners who, on a daily basis, perform complex analyses to gather necessary information for subsequent courtroom litigation. The educational skills of these practitioners range from the self-taught to those with doctoral degrees in applicable fields of analysis. However, multifaceted analyses can at times become overwhelming, particularly regarding differentiation of the techniques involved. For instance, consider the following real-case scenario:

> Several digital cameras at a convenience store allegedly capture an armed robbery of the store by several suspects. A hard drive from the video surveillance system is submitted to a computer forensics examiner for analysis. The hard drive contains 24 hours of multiplexed video. The investigator believes that somewhere on the hard drive is the video of the armed robbery. Along with the hard drive, the investigator submits a compact disk (CD) containing digital images of several potential suspects. The examiner is requested to analyze the hard drive, find the video of the armed robbery, capture and enhance the video images of the robbery suspects, and compare those images to the ones provided on the CD. Furthermore, the examiner is also requested to decipher, if possible, what the suspects said during the armed robbery.

This scenario raises all sorts of questions: "What type of analysis will the examiner be performing?" "Do we know for sure if the examiner will be performing computer analysis, video analysis, audio analysis, imaging analysis, or all four?" "Does the examiner have sufficient training?" "What is the experience level of the examiner?" "Where did the examiner obtain the necessary tools?" "Have they been validated and/or verified?" "What type of standards and controls will be used during the analysis?" The scenario depicts the need for conformity or uniformity in defining, handling, and examining digital and multimedia evidence. Evidentiary items may include both analog and digital media and/or the information contained therein. For practicality purposes, digital and multimedia analysis can be grouped under one discipline, the Digital & Multimedia Evidence discipline. This discipline can be further broken down into at least four subdisciplines: Forensic Audio Analysis, Computer Forensics, Image Analysis, and Video Analysis.

Many national and international organizations, such as the Scientific Working Group on Digital Evidence (SWGDE), the International High Technology Crime Investigation Association (HTCIA), the Digital Forensic Research Workshop (DFRWS), the Institute of Computer Forensic Professionals (ICFP), and the International Organization on Computer Evidence (IOCE) exist to provide guidance and leadership to the practitioners of the discipline. Furthermore, journals such as the *International Journal of Digital Evidence*, the *International Journal of Digital Forensics & Incident Response*, and others provide a forum for the dissemination of technical information. Other print media, such as *Forensic Magazine*, contain articles that discuss relevant topics. Organizations such as the International Association of Computer Investigative Specialists (IACIS) offer certifications to examiners to help ensure reliable analytical results. Even with this wealth of available resources, there continues to be one constant need in this emerging field that is not likely to change: an overview of the major elements of the discipline itself. Until now, there has been no one general source or reference that ties together such diverse topics as:

- The foundation of the discipline, analog and digital data
- How the Internet and Internet-related crime has affected our society
- The applicable laws on search and seizure
- What educational skills and training are needed to become an examiner
- Certification and accreditation
- Information security in the private and governmental sector
- How to investigate cybercrime
- How to collect evidence at a typical crime scene
- The types of digital and multimedia analysis performed
- Preparation for courtroom testimony.

This book, *Handbook of Digital and Multimedia Forensic Evidence*, was put together with the intent to be that reference. It can serve as a foundation and guide for (a) students considering a career in this field, (b) the law enforcement investigator assigned to work cybercrimes, (c) establishing training programs for forensic examiners, (d) the IT professional, (e) the veteran forensic examiner, and (f) the prosecutor faced with litigating cybercrime cases brought before a trier of fact. Because there is not any one person who is totally knowledgeable in all of these topics, a distinguished group of authors was selected to write individual chapters to address his or her specific areas of expertise. After reading this book and knowing that technology, techniques, and analyses change literally week to week, the reader will not become an "expert" in this field but rather will come away with a greater understanding of this multifaceted discipline.

John J. Barbara

Contents

Contributors

Rebecca Gurley Bace
Infidel, Inc.
Scotts Valley, California

Philip Craiger
National Center for Forensic Science
Department of Engineering Technology
University of Central Florida
Orlando, Florida

Philippe Dubord
Tampa, Florida

Erin E. Kenneally
University of California San Diego
San Diego Supercomputer Center
La Jolla, California

Larry R. Leibrock
Office of Deputy Secretary of Defense
Joint Improvised Explosive
Device Defeat Organization
Austin, Texas

Mark M. Pollitt
Digital Evidence Professional Services, Inc.
Ellicott City, Maryland

Donald Justin Price
Former Computer Forensic Examiner
for the Florida Department of Law Enforcement
Boyertown, Pennsylvania

Fred Chris Smith
Santa Fe, New Mexico

Chapter 1

The Analog and Digital World

Donald Justin Price

Summary

Digital devices shape every aspect of our lives—from online banking to ordering milk when your refrigerator detects you are low. These advances in technologies have been used to advance and improve our daily lives and, truly, the way in which we live. Unfortunately, these advances also have a dark side. Electronic devices are the new weapons of choice used by today's criminals. These activities range from sophisticated network intrusion to money laundering to exploiting children. Criminals attempt to hide behind digital zeros and ones in an effort to protect their identities while exploiting the identities of others. It is the responsibility of law enforcement and corporate America to understand digital devices and how to uncover a criminal's true identity through specialized training, sophisticated software, and a little bit of luck.

This chapter will introduce you to the world of digital information. It will briefly describe the basic fundamentals of digital and analog devices. It is not the intent of this chapter to cover every aspect of digital devices but rather to present a solid foundation of understanding for further detailed study of the subject matter. Let us start from the beginning; understanding the impact of mathematics.

Key Words: Bitmap, Bits, Bytes, MD-5, Partition, Sectors.

1. THE BINARY WORLD

Digital information is represented by two states; "0" or "1." This representation of two states is referred to as *binary*. Let us take a quick look at how binary digits are computed and how they are used to represent human-recognizable characters, numbers, and symbols. Each binary digit, "0" or "1," is called a *bit*. A bit is the smallest unit processed by digital devices. In order to represent more than two possibilities, digital information is combined into 8 bits, termed a *byte*. Each of the 8 bits has a specific

From: *Handbook of Digital and Multimedia Forensic Evidence*
Edited by: J. J. Barbara © Humana Press Inc., Totowa, NJ

Bit Position:	8th	7th	6th	5th	4th	3rd	2nd	1st
Value:	128	64	32	16	8	4	2	1

Fig. 1. Value placement within a byte.

value associated with its position. The value assigned to each bit increases from right to left, by a multiple of two (Fig. 1).

There are a total of 2^8, or 256, possible combinations within a byte. The American Standard Code for Information Interchange (ASCII) is a coding-based system that is used to represent characters, numbers, and various symbols. Each ACSII value has an assigned byte combination, totaling 256 possible characters, numbers, and symbols. When referencing an ASCII conversion chart, it is helpful to convert the binary digits into a decimal (base 10) or hexadecimal (base 16) value. How is this conversion accomplished?

Presume that we want to convert the following byte, "01010110," into a decimal value. Each bit has a specific value associated with its position. As you move from right to left, the bit's value becomes more significant. If the binary value is a "1," then the value assigned to that placeholder is added. If the binary value is a "0," then nothing is added. Now that we have all of the values assigned to each bit, all we have to do is add them together and get a decimal value of 86 (Fig. 2). Referencing an ACSII conversion chart, we note that the decimal value of 86 represents the capital letter "V."

Now let us look at converting the same byte into a hexadecimal value. When converting binary to hexadecimal, you first have to break the byte into two 4-bit segments. This 4-bit segment is called a *nibble*. Each bit within the nibble has a specific assigned value, just like the decimal conversion. Combining the values of each nibble yields the hexadecimal conversion (Fig. 3). Referencing an ASCII table, the hexadecimal value of 56 represents the capital letter "V," just as we expected from the previous example. In a hexadecimal system (base 16), the possible values are from 0 to 9 and A through F, "A" being equal to 10, "B" being equal to 11, and continuing until "F" equals 16. So why do we use hexadecimal to represent digital information? We do so simply because it takes less space to represent a single character, number, or symbol. Each hexadecimal value represents four binary values.

Byte:	0	1	0	1	0	1	1	0
Bit Value:	128	64	32	16	8	4	2	1
Conversion:	0	64	0	16	0	4	2	0
Decimal Value (86):		+64		+16		+4	+2	

Fig. 2. Converting a byte to a decimal value.

Byte:	0	1	0	1	0	1	1	0
Bit Value:	8	4	2	1	8	4	2	1
Conversion:	0	4	0	1	0	4	2	0
		+4		+1		+4	+2	
Hexadecimal Value:			5				6	

Fig. 3. Converting a byte to a hexadecimal value.

2. DIGITAL RECORDING

Now that we have a very general understanding of the binary world, let us explore how this information is stored on magnetic devices, such as hard drives, floppy diskettes, tapes, and so forth. Magnetic storage is based on the physics of magnetism. The magnetic storage device determines the magnetic property of each particle on a medium. The particle is either positively or negatively charged. As defined above, this is a true binary system. For example, a hard drive consists of platters, actuator arms, and read/write heads. The platters are normally made of aluminum or glass, which cannot flex. These platters contain a magnetic coating, which is used for data storage. Three popular types of magnetic coatings are oxide media, thin-film media, and antiferromagnetically coupled (AFC) media *(1)*. As the read/write head(s) of the hard drive move over each magnetic particle, the polarization of the particle will generate a pulse. Based on the particle's magnetic orientation between the read/write head, the particle will generate a positive or negative pulse. This is a very simple and basic description of how magnetic particles are converted into binary "0" and "1."

Binary information is stored on magnetic devices in areas called *sectors*. A sector is the smallest physical unit that can be used to store digital information. Each sector contains 512 bytes of storage space. The physical size of a sector is slightly larger, however; addressing information and error checking consumes a portion of the storage space. Sectors are organized in centric circles called *tracks*. The density of the media determines how many sectors per track the media contains. For example, a floppy diskette may have between 8 and 36 sectors per track; a higher density hard drive may have 900 or more sectors per track *(2)*. There are two recording processes possible when the sectors and tracks are created during the formatting process. These recording types are referred to as *standard* and *zone* recording. The standard recording process creates the same number of sectors per track across the entire magnetic device. This creates a major loss of data storage and an overall decrease in efficiency. In other words, you would have the same number of sectors per track on the innermost circles as you would on the outermost circles. This inefficiency led to the development of zone recording. When zone recording is used, there is an increased number of sectors per track within each track as you move out from the center of the medium.

Each storage unit on a magnetic device must have an address so that the hard drive knows where to find the data being requested. As magnetic devices have become more advanced and larger capacities are demanded, the number of addressable sectors has clearly approached its limit. Each storage unit is identified by using a set number of bits. The number of bits used in the address scheme is determined by how the medium is formatted. The formatting process prepares the medium for data storage and is accomplished within three steps: low-level format, partitioning, and high-level format. The low-level formatting process physically creates the tracks and divides them into sectors. Each sector is given its location address, and the data area is filled with test values *(3)*. The partitioning phase creates partitions on the medium. This allows multiple filing systems and/or operating systems to coexist. The last and final stage is the high-level format, which creates the infrastructure needed to properly manage the files that will be stored on the drive. This entire process is analogous to a new housing development. Several acres of land are parceled, streets are created, and appropriately sized lots for new homes are established. If needed, several subdivisions are created, one being for upscale homes, one for townhomes, one for single-family dwellings, and so forth. Finally, the homes are constructed in order to manage all of the families that live within the same community. Let us look at an example of how the formatting process affects data storage. A FAT16 formatted system uses a 16-bit value to address each storage unit. Therefore, there are a total of 65,536 addressable storage units. This limitation dictates that the largest maximum volume size cannot exceed 2 gigabytes. On the other hand, a FAT32 formatted system uses 32 bits for addressing storage units. Therefore, a total maximum volume size of 4 terabytes is theoretically possible *(4)*. A cluster, or allocation unit, is a group of one or more sectors on a disk. This represents the smallest logical unit in which data can be stored. Figure 4 illustrates an example of standard recording. In this formatting scheme, each cluster is made up of four sectors. Therefore, the smallest allocation unit assigned to any file is 2048 bytes.

    In the binary world, all types of files are stored magnetically in this fashion: programming codes, Microsoft Word documents, sound files, and video files.. It is the function of the operating system and program(s) to interrupt the ones and zeros as they are being generated by the read/write heads of the hard disk. Let us look at an example of a bitmap graphics file. In a bitmap graphics file, each byte represents specific intensities of the three primary colors, red, green, and blue (RGB). Therefore,

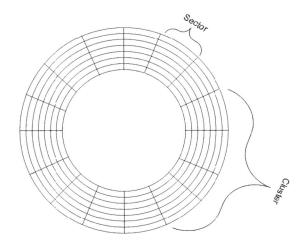

Fig. 4. Example of a cluster.

each RGB value contains 3 bytes, each byte representing an intensity of color *(5)*. Previously discussed was the concept of a byte; it consists of 8 bits. Each of the bits has a predetermined value associated with its location. The bit farthest to the left is called the *most significant bit*, because it has a value of 128. In contrast, the bit farthest to the right is the *least significant bit*, because its predetermined value is 1.

When a bitmap image is called by a program, the program will interpret each byte being generated by the hard drive's read/write heads. The programming code will know to read each byte and display the appropriate intensity of RGB and therefore produce an image that represents the collection of millions of these bytes. Figure 5 shows examples of the binary representation of three different common colors.

The technology of *steganography* takes advantage of this fact when concealing files within files. If a bitmap graphics file is used to conceal another file, the steganography program will replace the least significant bit within each byte. The file size of the original bitmap does not change, and the degradation of the image is undetectable by the human eye.

Another area within magnetic recording deals with random versus linear recording. Hard drives, floppy diskettes, and zip diskettes benefit from random recording. This gives the read/write heads of the device control of where to store the data. The system tries to be as efficient as possible and tends to store files in the closest available spaces to the read/write heads. The other option is to store the files sequentially, assuming the space is available. This type of operation is known as random recording, being able to "jump" around the disk to store digital information. A magnetic tape is a good example of a device that uses linear recording. This process has a greater "overhead" when trying to read and write digital information. If the user requests data that is stored at the end of the tape, the device must forward the tape to the proper location, wasting valuable time.

Optical media differ from magnetic media in that optical media use the principles of light to read and write data as opposed to magnetism. Examples of common optical media would be compact disks (CDs) and digital versatile disks (DVDs). The type of polymer being used will dictate if a disk is writable and/or rewritable. When the recording phase of optical media is initiated, a laser light is used to scribe pits into the polymer material. As the laser light transverses the disk, the reflection of the laser light is calculated and converted into electrical pulses, which are interpreted as binary zeros and ones (Fig. 6). Just like in magnetic devices, density plays a critical role in determining how much data can be stored on any given disk. A DVD has a much higher density than a CD; therefore, it can store almost seven times the amount of data.

Binary Code:	RGB Value:	Displayed Color:
000000000000000000000000	0,0,0	Black
000000001111111100000000	0,255,0	Green
100000001000000010000000	128,128,128	Gray

Fig. 5. Examples of three common colors and their respective binary representation.

....0 1 1 0 0 1 0 0 1 1 0 0 1 0 0 1 0 0 1 1 0 0 ....

Polymer

Fig. 6. Profile view of the "lands" and "pits" as observed on optical media.

3. ANALOG RECORDING

Analog information is continuous; the transmitted signal is analogous to the original signal *(6)*. A sound wave is an example of an analog system. The intensity of the sound is directly proportional to the sound wave. Converting or recording analog information to its digital counterpart is called *digitizing*. In the conversion process, the analog sound waves are broken up into many pieces and converted into numbers and stored digitally (Fig. 7). The quality of the conversion process is directly affected by the rate of sampling. Naturally, a higher sampling frequency will generate a higher quality digital audio conversion. Each specific number generated from the recording phase is proportional to the voltage level during playback. Just like the RGB values of graphics files, the *bit value* plays an important role in audio files.

4. IMAGE ANALYSIS

Digital photography has been well accepted and embraced. The advances of digital cameras and their corresponding technology has become so mainstream that professional-grade cameras are within the price range of average consumers. With the proliferation of digital cameras in society, criminals have taken advantage of this technology. This has forced law enforcement to develop and refine techniques of image analysis. There is a definite need for comparing, enlarging, repairing, enhancing, and analyzing graphics files. With the advances of modern technology, we are able to accomplish each of these tasks with great precision and accuracy. Gone are the days of using magnifying glasses and destructive chemicals and processes to analyze

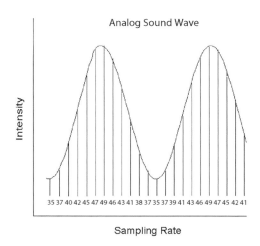

Fig. 7. Digitizing an audio sample.

000a0	20 20 20 20 20 20 20 20-20 20 20 20 20 20 20 20	
000b0	20 20 20 20 20 20 20 20-20 20 20 20 20 00 53 4f	·SO
000c0	4e 59 00 4d 56 43 2d 43-44 33 35 30 00 48 00 00	NY·MVC-CD350·H··
000d0	00 01 00 00 00 48 00 00-00 01 00 00 00 41 43 44	·····H·······ACD
000e0	20 53 79 73 74 65 6d 73-20 44 69 67 69 74 61 6c	Systems Digital
000f0	20 49 6d 61 67 69 6e 67-00 32 30 30 34 3a 30 38	Imaging·2004:08
00100	3a 32 38 20 31 37 3a 35-33 3a 30 36 00 1c 00 9a	:28 17:53:06····
00110	82 05 00 01 00 00 00 57-02 00 00 9d 82 05 00 01	·······W········
00120	00 00 00 5f 02 00 00 22-88 03 00 01 00 00 00 02	···_···"········
00130	00 00 00 27 88 03 00 01-00 00 00 a0 00 00 00 00	···'············
00140	90 07 00 04 00 00 00 30-32 32 30 03 90 02 00 14	·······0220·····

Fig. 8. Example of image header information.

images. Through research and software and technical developments, we are able to analyze these images and uncover their hidden past or true identity. A simple example of image analysis would be to determine the manufacturer and model number of a digital camera that captured a questioned photograph. Using a hex editor program, the image file's hexadecimal values can be examined. The beginning part of a file is called the *header information*. Various types of information can be contained within this area. Information such as file type (i.e., Microsoft Word document, JPEG, BMP, etc.), digital camera information, or program information could be extracted from the header information. Figure 8 shows an example of the header information within a digital photograph taken with a Sony Mavica CD-350 digital camera.

Of course, this is an extremely simple example of image analysis. More complex issues involved with image analysis include, among others, image enhancement, image authentication, comparison, and stereography detection. Major strides have been made to perfect this critical need within digital evidence. Sophisticated tools are capable of bit manipulation within the binary data in order to interpolate and enhance resolution of imagery.

Mathematical algorithms can be used to authenticate or compare images. MD-5 (Message Digest) is a standard algorithm used in digital evidence and could be used for comparing digital images. The MD-5 algorithm is a polynomial in which binary information is introduced that in turn generates a unique alphanumeric sequence. This MD-5 value can be accepted as a digital fingerprint of the data that was processed. The odds of any two files generating the same MD-5 hash value are roughly 1 in 3.4×10^{38}. Therefore, if two digital photographs need to be authenticated as being exact duplicates of each other, the file's binary information could be inserted into the MD-5 hash algorithm. If the alphanumeric values match, then you have reasonable certainty that the two digital photographs are identical. Keep in mind that this procedure could be used for any file type, not just digital photographs.

5. EFFECTS OF DIGITAL INFORMATION IN SOCIETY

As mentioned in the beginning of this chapter, digital information shapes every aspect of our lives. It seems we have become more reliant on digital information than on crude oil. National defense, utility infrastructure, business, and entertainment rely on digital information. In fact, most of these would not exist in their current forms without it. So what does this mean for you and me? As we become more dependent on digital information, it becomes even more important for us to understand the technology and defend it against individuals who choose to exploit and misuse the technology. Computers, smart phones, PDAs, and such are becoming smaller and more advanced yet, at the same time, increasing their capacity to store information. The discipline of digital evidence must constantly adapt and change with technological developments in order to be an effective front against digital crime. Digital technology is changing in four main areas: physical size, storage capacity, processing power, and data security. Let us take a look at each area and how it affects law enforcement and society.

5.1. Physical Size

From the Motorola razors to ultrathin laptops to the iPod nano, digital information can be stored anywhere. Individuals can be carrying gigabytes of digital information in their pockets, around their necks, or even in their watches. This should cause great concern for law enforcement and society itself. Criminals are now able to store their incriminating evidence on these (and other) small devices. Officers need to be properly trained to recognize that virtually any digital device can be/is capable of storing digital evidence. To avoid being arrested and prosecuted for a crime, one of a criminal's best defenses is the concealment of evidence. If the incriminating digital evidence is never found, charges could not be filed. One simple example of this could be an individual suspected of Internet fraud. The user's Internet activity would be crucial to their prosecution. If the suspect was using a U3 enabled thumb drive, all of the user's Internet activity would reside in the thumb drive, not on the computer itself. If the seizing agent never noticed the thumb drive, critical evidence could be lost forever. Training and experience is a critical piece to the puzzle. Any sworn law enforcement officer who executes search warrants should have a basic understanding of this technology and be able to recognize such critical pieces of evidence. As technology advances, digital storage devices will take on an array of shapes and sizes. Ink pens are no longer just ink pens and watches are no longer just watches. They should be thought of and treated as potential pieces of evidence.

5.2. Storage Capacity

The technology used to store digital information is also constantly changing. The industry demands not only smaller devices as mentioned above but also large storage capacities. Consumers want to be able to store entire music collections and family video footage without a concern for free space. With the advent and proliferation of digital cameras and digital video cameras, having a storage capacity of 500 gigabytes to 1000 gigabytes is not uncommon for the consumer. As technology of perpendicular recording becomes more prevalent, storage capacities are going to be increasing exponentially. This will place a certain burden on law enforcement. Digital evidence examiners will be required to make well-informed decisions when determining what information to capture, how to capture the information, and ultimately how to process the enormous amount of data. The art and science of digital forensics relies on the ability of the examiner to find the "needle in the haystack." However, as the needle gets smaller in size, the haystack is getting bigger.

5.3. Processing Power

Processing power is the only area that benefits the criminal as well as law enforcement. Being able to process more data per second will not only lower the total processing time but also will allow the examiner to find the data more efficiently. However, this becomes less effective as storage capacity continues to expand. In an ideal world, a computer's processing power would be directly proportional to its storage capacity. As we all know, our world is far from perfect.

5.4. Data Security

Password protection and encryption are examples of data security. Society must be mindful of personal information being stored on digital devices. Any digital information that could be exploited must be protected. Password protection and encryption only allow authorized users to access the protected information. Cryptography is the process of concealing the contents of a file from all except for authorized users. As cryptographers create more secure algorithms used in data encryption, others will be testing their vulnerabilities and exploiting any weakness. Encryption schemes and strong passwords are very effective ways of ensuring data security. This fact alone should impose great concern to law enforcement when processing digital evidence. It requires examiners to think "outside-the-box" when dealing with cases known to involve encryption. Basic encryption schemes need to be understood by examiners. This understanding will allow them to make sound decisions when seizing digital evidence. During the execution of a search warrant, just walking into a residence or business and "pulling-the-plug" on a computer is no longer a viable option. Seizing agents must be more mindful of encryption programs and must understand how to best deal with the technology in an already highly stressful situation. If left unchecked, valuable data could be lost forever. Remember, the main purpose of encryption is to conceal or secure data from unauthorized access. If the suspect is using encryption, you can bet that the critical data is secured. However, as encryption schemes become more secure, so does the technology used to circumvent the process. Code-breaking software is an indispensable tool to digital evidence examiners. A weak password or pass phrase coupled with the strongest encryption scheme is meaningless. "The chain is only as strong as its weakest link" is an effective principle to apply when using passwords. Code-breaking tools use this fact to exploit the entire process in order to recover the password and, ultimately, to read the decrypted file.

Encryption is a two-edged sword. Cryptographers are constantly striving to develop the world's perfect encryption algorithm. If such an algorithm exists or is even possible, the direct effect on our society could be detrimental. A "would-be" terrorist could use this "perfect" encryption algorithm to conceal their radical views and plans to commit terrorist acts against any person or country. For this reason, the computer industry, law enforcement, and intelligence agencies should strive to work together in an effort to improve software products and digital devices without tying the hands of law enforcement.

6. CONCLUSION

Law enforcement and society will always play a cat and mouse game when it comes to developing technology. As new digital devices are invented, their inherent weaknesses are determined and exploited. As a result, the developers start the building process all over again, which ultimately leads to a better and stronger product.

REFERENCES

[1] Mueller, S. (2002). *Upgrading and Repairing PCs*, 14th ed. Indianapolis: Que, p. 610.
[2] Ibid., p. 601.
[3] Ibid., pp. 604–608.
[4] Ibid., p. 607.
[5] Lewis, J., and Loftus W. (2005). *JAVA Software Solutions*, 4th ed.. New York: Pearson Education, Inc., p. 95.
[6] Newton, H. (2003). *Newton's Telecom Dictionary*, 19th ed. San Francisco: CMP Books, p. 61.

Chapter 2

Training and Education in Digital Evidence

Philip Craiger

Summary

Digital forensics is a relatively new science that is becoming increasingly important as tech-savvy criminals use computers and networks in their illegal activities. Demonstrated competency in digital forensics requires a varied knowledge and skill set that includes an in-depth understanding of computer hardware and software, computer networks, forensic science, applicable local, state, and national laws, as well as the ability to communicate in both verbal and written forms. The purpose of this chapter is to provide the reader with an overview of education and training in digital forensics. Issues specifically addressed include differences between education and training; the "core competencies" of the digital forensics examiner; guidelines on the knowledge and skills students should expect to learn in a college/university educational program; a description of various types of training programs; as well as pointers to Web resources for current information on available educational and training programs.

Key Words: Core competencies, Digital forensics, Examination plan, Hashing, IACIS, NW3C, Operating systems, SWGDE, TWGED.

1. INTRODUCTION

Law enforcement and business and industry increasingly encounter crimes that involve *digital evidence*. In 2000, the Scientific Working Group on Digital Evidence (SWGDE) defined digital evidence as "…any information of probative value that is stored or transmitted in a binary form" *(1)*. The new science of *digital forensics* is the application of science and technology to the identification, recovery, transportation, and storage of digital evidence. Digital forensics is a relatively new forensic science compared

From: *Handbook of Digital and Multimedia Forensic Evidence*
Edited by: J. J. Barbara © Humana Press Inc., Totowa, NJ

with biological (e.g., DNA) and physical-based (e.g., Gun Shut Residue (GSR), explosions, fingerprints, tool marks) forensics. Due to the ubiquity of digital media and its use in criminal activities, law enforcement, business, and industry, the forensic science community has become increasingly aware of the importance of digital forensics and the fact that it must be addressed as a profession and a science given its importance in many court cases. Accordingly, it is crucial that those involved in the recovery, examination, and preservation of digital evidence have the requisite training and education to deal effectively with the growing amount of evidence they will encounter.

The reader is presented with two caveats concerning this chapter. First, technology changes quickly—technologies become obsolete, and new technologies are created on an almost daily basis. These changes have a significant effect upon the practice of digital forensics, making it a "moving" target that requires practitioners to update their knowledge and skills to remain current of these changes. The second caveat concerns existing educational and training programs. Discussions of specific educational and training programs in this chapter are intentionally limited as they change on a regular basis. Discussions of specific vendor-supplied training and university programs would make this chapter essentially obsolete or incomplete by the time of publication. Consequently, in this chapter the focus is upon the fundamentals of digital forensics (i.e., principles, procedures, knowledge, and skills that are likely to be important for the foreseeable future). The reader can then use this information to compare and contrast university educational programs and training programs to determine the extent to which these programs meet these criteria. Discussed are a limited number of training programs that have been in existence for some time and most likely should continue to be in existence for years to come. Included at the end of this chapter are links to Web-based resources that are updated on a regular basis and that the readers can use to identify programs of interest.

2. TRAINING VERSUS EDUCATION

People often confuse the terms *training* and *education*. Although definitions of the two often appear to be similar (compare Merriam-Webster's online dictionary for the definitions of *educate* and *train*), for the purposes of this chapter they are treated as generally distinct concepts that are not interchangeable but rather complementary. The primary distinction for this chapter is that (good) educational programs, offered at colleges and universities, provide knowledge and skills as a means of *developing a student's general problem-solving skills*. Thus, educational programs focus on instilling *fundamental knowledge and skills* revolving around a particular subject. There are also distinctions between undergraduate and graduate university programs. Students in an undergraduate program are exposed to a breadth of topics and experiences, whereas graduate programs (master's and doctoral programs) are more focused in scope and require a greater level of mastery of subject matter. Graduate programs usually involve a research component where the student must demonstrate their mastery of a subject or a particular problem through the creation of new knowledge about a subject.

Students in computer-related university degree programs may use software tools to demonstrate their understanding of the subject matter; however, students are expected to be able to demonstrate this understanding using other tools that were not discussed during the course and to apply the knowledge and skills required to problems that the student might not have encountered during the course. Because of the diversity and depth of technology-related problems, students often participate in internships, during or after their degree, to expand their knowledge and skill sets.

Training programs, in contrast, are typically focused on procedural knowledge (i.e., how to complete a task in step-by-step fashion). Whereas educational programs are broader in focus, a typical training program focuses on a targeted set of knowledge and skills and is usually of short duration (a few days to a few weeks). Technology-related training programs also tend to have a heavy hands-on component, where students work directly with software tools to develop a level of competency with the tools.

3. THE DIGITAL FORENSICS EXAMINER

There are a number of positions (jobs) in which someone with a background (experience and/or education) in digital forensics may be competent to serve. The most common position that is relevant for this chapter is the position of a *digital forensics examiner*. FBI Special Agent Mark Pollitt (retired), former director of the FBI's Computer Analysis Response Team and manager of the FBI's Regional Computer Forensics Labs, defined a digital forensic examiner as

> …[someone who] forensically acquires, preserves, examines and presents information stored or transmitted in binary form which may be probative in a legal context. They may (or may not) conduct investigative analysis *(2)*.

Although the actual title of *digital forensics examiner* is more likely to be found in law enforcement, parties in industry perform these same tasks under varying names, as well as consultants who freelance on case-by-base basis.

The job of digital forensics examiners requires a varied knowledge and skill set. A competent examiner must be able to exhibit a technical understanding of various types of computer hardware, computer networks, operating systems, file systems, and various types of application software; an understanding of local, state, and federal laws that may come into play during the computer-related crime investigation; the ability to write a detailed report of the procedures used and the findings of the examination in both a technical and nontechnical manner; and finally to be able to accurately testify to the findings in a court of law to a jury of laypersons. Very few existing college/university programs (as of mid-2007) offer a comprehensive package of courses that encompasses this varied knowledge and skill set.

As mentioned previously, at the end of this chapter there are Web references where the reader may find specific information about educational programs that offer a degree or courses in digital forensics. Rather than including a list of educational programs in this chapter, which would become out-of-date within a short period of time, the knowledge, skills, and abilities (KSAs) that an examiner must exhibit in order to be assessed as competent or proficient are presented for review. It is suggested that readers interested in participating in an educational degree program use this list as a guideline for comparison with educational offerings to determine the appropriateness of the degree or courses to fit the need of the individual.

3.1. Core Competencies

In 2005, subject matter experts from private industry, academia, and the government developed a consensus model of the core competencies (i.e., KSAs) that a digital forensics examiner must exhibit to be deemed "competent" in the field. These subject matter experts serve as the Development Committee of the Digital Forensics Certification Board, whose task is to ensure and maintain quality assurance in the field of digital forensics.

The committee identified five core competencies related to determining *competency* in digital forensics. These competencies are partitioned according to the primary tasks that an examiner encounters. From a broad perspective, these general tasks include:

- The ability to identify and transport media that may contain evidence.
- The ability to create a forensically sound copy of the media and validate it, as well as preview the media without altering its contents.
- Given various criteria, the ability to recover evidence meeting the criteria.
- The ability to make interpretations and inferences regarding the recovered evidence.
- The ability to effectively and accurately testify in a court as to the interpretations.

A college/university educational program may have one to several courses that cover in varying levels of detail the knowledge and skills underlying these tasks. A course that covers the entire spectrum of competencies will not cover them at a depth that one would find in a program that covers the same competencies in several courses. Each of these core competencies will be described in more detail. Additionally, information is provided on the expectations that prospective students should have with regard to the types of topics and projects that courses should include to provide the student with sufficient coverage of the core competency.

3.1.1. Acquiring Potential Evidence

It is critical that examiners be able to identify all digital devices that are capable of storing potential evidence. This list includes internal computer hard drives, external hard drives, USB thumb drives, flash memory cards, CDs, DVDs, cell phones, PDAs, floppy disks, wireless network access points, game consoles (Sony's PSP and Microsoft's XBOX, for example), and so on. USB thumb drives are an interesting case because they come in many form factors, for instance, some resemble Pez dispensers, Swiss Army knives, wrist watches, and even Sushi. An inexperienced responder would easily overlook these "interesting" devices.

After identifying the media, the examiner must be able to create a "forensically" sound copy of the media without changing the contents of the media. (A forensically sound copy is a bit-for-bit copy of the media, i.e., an exact physical duplicate.) The examiner must be able to demonstrate these procedures at the scene of the crime directly, over a network, and in the lab if the media has been seized.

It is crucial that the examiner does not violate any applicable laws during the process of recovering media. An examiner must demonstrate knowledge of warrants, consent, discovery orders and subpoenas, and the relationship to decisions of what to acquire. This is crucial as any laws, either intentionally or inadvertently, violated by the examiner may lead to the exclusion of the evidence by a judge, which has led to dismissals of cases.

An examiner may have to open a computer to have direct access to the hard disk, to determine how many drives are installed, and to determine if any evidence is hidden inside the computer. The examiner must understand how to identify specific computer settings, such as serial numbers, jumper settings on a hard drive, network card identifiers (MAC addresses), and so on.

The examiner must understand how to examine the contents of the media at the scene to determine if any evidence is contained on the media, often called an *onsite preview*. Students must be able to demonstrate an understanding of quality assurance and quality controls that are essential to forensic sciences, including knowledge of standard protocols and how to develop standard operating procedures; how to validate a software tool; and how to validate findings.

3.1.1.1. STUDENT EXPECTATIONS

At a minimum, students should be exposed to several projects that require them to create an image of a piece of digital media, preferably several types of media, such as a hard drive, a floppy disk, a USB thumb drive, and a CD or DVD. Students should have to verify/validate the forensic copies using a hashing algorithm. They also should be exposed to many types of media of varying form factor, although not necessarily in a project format, and to be able to identify them and understand the issues involved in creating forensic copies of the media. Students should also be able to demonstrate an understanding of how to identify various hardware components, as well as computer settings including BIOS settings, network configurations, user account information, and so forth. Finally, students should be exposed to case scenarios that involve warrants, consent, discovery orders and subpoenas, and be able to demonstrate an understanding of the limitations of their work given these legal documents.

3.1.2. Examination

The purpose of a forensic examination is to identify potential evidence located on digital media. Given the diversity of digital evidence, a competent examiner must understand the technologies and applications; where information is stored, in what format it is stored, and any special procedures that may be required for recovering the information (e.g., information that may be encrypted in a binary format and is therefore human unreadable without translation to a human-readable format). Common applications and technologies that must be understood include networking and communications technologies; peer-to-peer applications; e-mail; instant messaging; and Web browsers (e.g., browser cache files, Internet history files, and cookies). Examiners must exhibit an understanding of multiple versions of each type of application, for instance, there are several popular Web browsers, each of which stores information in a slightly different format and location on a hard drive.

Examiners should understand various types of special files that may be located on media, including how to identify and translate it if required. These special files include malware (viruses, worms, bots, and keystroke loggers); files obfuscated through encryption, steganography, or compression, and secure deletion programs. Students should be exposed to each of these types of special files and demonstrate an understanding of the difficulties in dealing with these files as well as various ways of overcoming them (e.g., ways of recovering passwords to encrypted files).

Examiners must be familiar with a variety of tools, including the commercial as well as open source software tools. Common examination tasks to recover evidence include creating digital fingerprints of files to authenticate or ensure data integrity (commonly called *hashing*); searching for files using various criteria including keywords, date and time stamps, file types to reduce the data; recovering "deleted" files; and understanding the concept of *data ownership* and history. Students should be required to use one, if not several, different tools in hands-on assignments to create file hashes; identify specific files using various criteria; recover a deleted file; and demonstrate how to identify a file's owner.

Competent examiners are familiar with more than one operating system and file system. Students should also be exposed to multiple operating systems (e.g., Windows, Linux, Mac OS X), as well as different versions of operating systems (e.g., Windows 98, Windows XP, Windows NT) because of large differences in how some operating systems work. Students should be exposed to multiple flavors of file systems (e.g., FAT, NTFS, Linux EXT2/3, Hierarchical File System) as these file systems have distinct methods of file creation, storage, retrieval, and deletion.

Examiners must understand the difference between a logical and physical analysis of digital media as well as demonstrate what types of information can be gathered from each. Logical-level data views data from the viewpoint of a file system and includes all files that are currently allocated and tracked by the file system (this does not include deleted files). Physical-level data views storage media as one large file and includes allocated files as well as deleted files and file slack. Students should be required to complete both a logical and a physical analysis of digital media. Students must also be able to demonstrate an understanding of metadata that is associated with files, such as data and time stamps, file size, file ownership, file name, as well as at an application level (e.g., word processing documents typically contain information on the author, last date of modification, and related information).

Examiners may encounter a running computer that cannot be turned off for some reason (e.g., a network intruder has broken into the computer and is still logged in or the company will not allow the examiner to turn the computer off). In these instances, the examiner must understand where "live" data is located and how to recover that information. For instance, the contents of RAM, current network connections, current running processes, and so on may contain evidentiary information crucial to an investigation. Students should be exposed to numerous hands-on projects where they encounter a live system and must recover evidence of varying levels of volatility, including the contents of RAM, network information, and running processes.

Competent examiners have a "game plan" for their examination. Before conducting an examination, an examiner creates an examination plan that describes the types of information to be recovered as well as the procedures that will be used in the recovery. Therefore, examiners must have a working knowledge of standard operating procedures, protocols, and examination documentation. In all assignments involving examinations, students should be required to develop a written examination plan that details the order of the procedures that they will execute. The instructor should expose students to assignments where they create an examination plan and demonstrate the ability to follow standard operating procedures and protocols as provided. This should be started early-on in the program as this is a crucial concept in the forensic sciences. Instructors should require students to write up, in a standard format, the results of each examination conducted. Students should use this standard format for all of their assignment write-ups, beginning early in the program.

3.1.2.1. STUDENT EXPECTATIONS

Whenever possible, students should be exposed to a variety of commercial tools. Demonstration versions of some commercial tools are available if the cost of the full tool is prohibitive. Additionally, students should be exposed to open source tools for a variety of operating systems (e.g., http://www.opensourceforensics.org/tools/) and be able to use them to recover evidence, validate the tools, and understand the limitations of the tools. Students should be exposed to the most prevalent operating systems (Windows and Linux at a minimum) and file systems (FAT, NTFS, and EXT2/3 at a minimum). Students should be able to demonstrate an understanding of the fundamental differences between the different types of operating systems and file systems. Additionally, students should be exposed to projects that require them to recover evidence from different operating systems and different file systems. Students should be able to conduct both physical and logical analyses and be able to demonstrate what types of evidence each are capable of recovering.

3.1.3. Analysis

The final set of knowledge and skills involves an understanding of law and procedures, investigative as well as technical analytical practices. It is crucial that an examiner have a broad investigative awareness of the circumstances surrounding a case as this may dictate the types of evidence of importance to a case. It is also important that an examiner understand what they do not know about a case and know where to go to gather information that may assist in identifying and recovering evidence. Therefore, it is important that a student in a university program be exposed to somewhat realistic case scenarios that require an investigative element as opposed to simply rote evidence recovery. This will enable students to become familiar with the investigative process.

As digital forensics examinations occur within a legal context, it is imperative that examiners (and students) are familiar with criminal and civil laws and procedures. Students should become familiar with the Fourth Amendment to the U.S. Constitution; differences between workplace and public workplace searches; searches and seizures without a warrant; the Electronic Communications and Privacy Act (and amendments); and electronic surveillance in communications networks (usually referred to as Title III). A good source of materials for this is the U.S. Department of Justice's *Manual for Searching and Seizing Computers and Obtaining Electronic Evidence in Criminal Investigations*, developed by the Computer Crime and Intellectual Property Section, Criminal Division (http://www.usdoj.gov/criminal/cybercrime/s&smanual2002.htm).

Examiners are more than just evidence gatherers. They must also be able to draw inferences and conclusions based on the evidence they find. Examiners must be able to identify the sources of e-mails, instant messages, and other communications. Cases may require the placement of events on a timeline and the examiner explaining how the operating and file systems allocate date and time stamps. Examiners must be able to attribute, within reason, digital artifacts to a particular user, locations, or events. Students should be exposed to multiple hands-on projects in which they are required to identify sources of communications and to draw inferences regarding the timeline of communications between multiple sources based on time and date stamps.

Digital evidence displays varying levels of volatility. For example, the contents of RAM will disappear once the computer is powered-down, and all network-related information will be lost as well. Recovering volatile evidence is possible, however the act of recovering the evidence will in most cases alter the contents of the evidence. This is particularly true of RAM. In contrast, the contents of a hard drive are fairly stable and the contents of CD-ROMs and DVDs are in generally immutable. Examiners must understand where potential evidence may reside on a running computer and determine the appropriateness of powering down a computer. Students should be exposed to digital media of varying levels of volatility and be able to demonstrate an understanding of the trade-offs of recovering each source of information.

3.1.3.1. STUDENT EXPECTATIONS

Students must demonstrate an understanding of civil privacy laws, especially regarding policies and procedures governing personal information. Coverage should include Health Information Portability and Privacy Act (http://www.hhs.gov/ocr/hipaa/), Gramm-Leach-Bliley Act (http://www.ftc.gov/privacy/privacyinitiatives/glbact.htm), Electronic Communications Privacy Act, Personal Privacy Act of 1974 (http://www.epic.org/privacy/laws/privacy_act.html), and others. Students should be exposed to various scenarios in which they apply their knowledge of the laws outlined above in order to demonstrate their understanding of the effect of legal precedents on the tasks they would perform as an examiner.

For each project, students should include in their examination plan a description of what information is being sought as well as the procedures that will be used in the recovery of that information. Each project should require a two-part written report. The part that describes the findings would be written for nontechnical persons such as judges, juries, and attorneys. The second part would be written at a more technical level and would include the examination plan. The level of detail of the second section should be written such that another examiner could use the report to accurately replicate the procedures and findings of the examiner (student).

Students should be exposed to various communication applications (e-mail, Web browsers, instant messaging, peer-to-peer, etc.) and be able to demonstrate how these applications function, where application-relevant information (configuration, log files, downloaded files) is stored, and how to recover these files. Additionally, students should be able to use date and time stamps along with application-specific information to create a timeline that illustrates the timeline of communications occurring between end users.

3.2. Summary

Competent digital forensic examiners must exhibit a depth and breadth of knowledge and skill sets. Those interested in a digital forensics educational program should use the core competencies described above as guidelines and compare them with the contents of courses offered in university programs. The guidelines provided are just that—guidelines. They were developed from experience in our own courses and from knowledge of others who teach similar courses. The courses that follow these guidelines may provide students with a well-rounded and comprehensive educational experience.

4. EDUCATIONAL PROGRAMS AND CRITERIA

The Technical Working Group on Training and Education in Digital Evidence (TWGED) was a collection of experts from business/industry, law enforcement, and academia whose objective was to develop criteria and model training and educational programs in the science of digital forensics. The result is a document, to be published by the National Institute of Justice, which provides prospective students, universities, and industry with guidelines (suggestions) on the contents of model programs. Model programs are included for associate, bachelor, and graduate levels, as well as continuing education and training programs. The reader is referred to this document (when published) to find more specific information on the model programs.

The TWGED identified a series of knowledge, skills, and abilities (KSAs) that a student should encounter in a model digital forensics educational program. These KSAs were divided into two categories: technical and professional. For the technical aspects, students must become familiar with computer hardware and architecture; storage media; operating systems; file systems; database systems; network technologies and infrastructures; programming and scripting; computer security; cryptography; software tools; validation and testing; and cross-discipline awareness.

In addition, the group developed professional criteria that include critical thinking; scientific methodology; quantitative reasoning and problem solving; decision making; laboratory practices; laboratory safety; attention to detail; interpersonal skills; public speaking; oral and written communications; time management; task prioritization; application of digital forensic procedures; preservation of evidence; interpretation of examination results; investigative process; and legal process.

Mastering many of the professional topics differentiates an educational program in digital forensics from a training program.

4.1. Existing Educational Programs

As of mid-2007 there are few undergraduate or graduate degrees in digital forensics or computer forensics. Some universities offer digital forensics as either a major or minor; for example, a degree in computer science, information technology, or engineering technology with a major/minor in computer forensics. A major usually requires students to take a series of related courses amounting to approximately 15 to 20 hours of coursework. Minors are usually composed of three to four courses for somewhere between 9 and 12 hours.

Several community colleges have begun to offer associates' degrees in computer forensics. Associates' programs are composed of approximately 60 hours of coursework. Several universities are offering graduate certificates in computer forensics. Graduate certificate programs may be perfect for those who desire a more "compact" version of a program without requiring them to participate in a full 30- to 36-hour master's program or requiring them to take (retake) the Graduate Record Examination. Graduate certificate programs range from four to six courses composing from 12 to 18 hours of courses. These courses usually include technical courses, legal courses, and perhaps a general course in forensic science.

The most up-to-date information about community college/university information on computer forensics degree programs can be found online at http://www.e-evidence.info/education.html.

5. TRAINING PROGRAMS

Training programs typically fall along a number of continuums. For instance, some teach the fundamentals of digital forensics (identification, preservation, storage, analysis, and legal aspects), whereas others are primarily software tool–related and are provided by a software vendor. A few training programs fall somewhere in between: they teach fundamentals as well as selected software tools. Some training programs are for law enforcement only, whereas others support business/industry, consultants, as well as law enforcement. Finally, some training programs (primarily law enforcement) are provided free of charge, whereas others can be quite expensive, especially when a vendor requires purchase of their product in order to participate in the class. The cost of training is additional to the cost of the software.

Below are described some existing training programs that are available to law enforcement only. They are specifically mentioned because they have been in existence for many years and most likely will be in existence for the foreseeable future. At the end of this chapter, we provide links to Web resources that provide information on existing vendor-based training programs.

5.1. Law Enforcement–Only Training

One of the older training providers is the National White Collar Crime Center (NW3C; www.nw3c.org). NW3C is a nonprofit corporation whose membership is composed of law enforcement agencies, state regulatory bodies with criminal investigative authority, and state and local prosecution offices. Over the past 24 years, NW3C has offered dozens of courses of widely varying content, including courses useful for a probation officer; regarding financial crimes; regarding terrorism; as well as several courses that cover the technical aspects of digital forensics. These law enforcement–only courses are free of charge and held at various sites throughout the United States.

The International Association of Computer Investigative Specialists (IACIS; www.iacis.info) offers several training courses to members of law enforcement. According to their Web site, IACIS is an international volunteer nonprofit corporation composed of law enforcement professionals from federal, state, local, and international law enforcement agencies. These law enforcement–only courses are usually held once a year in Orlando, Florida. There are costs associated with the training.

The High Technology Crime Investigation Association (HTCIA; www.htcia.org) is an international organization whose purpose is to "…encourage, promote, aid and effect the voluntary interchange of data, information, experience, ideas and knowledge about methods, processes, and techniques relating to investigations and security in advanced technologies among its membership." Its membership is open to local, state, or federal government officials who are involved in the investigation of electronic crimes. HTCIA provides training programs to its members several times throughout the year.

National law enforcement agencies, including the FBI and the U.S. Secret Service, have developed their own training programs for agents and officers. These programs range from basic courses in understanding how computer hardware and software works to advanced courses such as network intrusions. These are comprehensive courses that are open to agents of the individual agency providing the training, although some seats may be made available to local and state law enforcement agents.

5.2. Vendor Training

Digital forensics software development companies (AKA vendors) may offer training in their tools. Examples of vendors who also provide training include (in alphabetical order) AccessData (www.accessdata.com), ASR Data (www.asrdata.com), Digital Intelligence (www.digitalintelligence.com), and Guidance Software (www.guidancesoftware.com). Vendor-provided training is open to law enforcement, business/industry, consultants, and any other interested parties. Training is held in various locations in the United States and some internationally. Costs range according to the vendor and specific course, and some vendors require the purchase of their software before an interested party can participate in the training.

Vendor training may last from one day to a week or more, depending upon the depth of the course. Vendors usually offer more than one course (e.g., beginning, intermediate, and advanced courses). The author is familiar with many of the courses taught by these vendors, and the courses are usually comprehensive and provide numerous hands-on projects during the course.

During these courses, participants are provided descriptions of the software, its functionality, as well as instructor-led demonstrations of how to use a particular aspect of the software. Participants are usually provided digital media (e.g., hard drive images) to practice using the software tool and to demonstrate proficiency in the use of the tool. Training programs tend to concentrate on procedural knowledge, that is, how to use the tool in a step-by-step fashion in order to accomplish a specific task.

5.3. Training and Certification

Several vendors and training organizations provide "certifications." A certification essentially indicates that the holder of the certification has demonstrated proficiency in the procedures and tools that were included as part of the training. Most vendors provide a "certificate of completion" at the end of the course; however, this should not be construed as a "certification." A true "certification" usually requires a hands-on practicum that is completed off-site; a written report that documents the procedures the participant used to complete the practicum as well as any findings; and often includes a written examination. The cost of certification is over and above the cost of training a participant may have incurred. Certifying bodies may require a certified member to participate and document continuing education, and perhaps complete regular proficiency exams and dues payment, in order to remain current in the certification.

One certification body of note is IACIS, which offers two certifications, Certified Electronic Evidence Collection Specialist Certification (CEECS) and Certified Forensic Computer Examiner (CFCE). There are a number of commercial vendor certifications, too numerous to mention here. Vendor certifications require a hands-on practicum as well as a test. These certifications also require ongoing renewal, either through a demonstration of continuing education (training) credits or through additional proficiency exams (see Chapter 3).

6. WEB-BASED RESOURCES

Educational programs and training programs built around technology change quickly. Moreover, programs, in particular training programs, tend to come and go. In order to provide more up-to-the-minute information about educational and training programs, the following resources are available:

1. To learn more about educational and training programs:

   - http://www.e-evidence.info/education.html
   - http://dir.yahoo.com/Computers_and_Internet/Forensics/
   - http://www.education-online-search.com/programs/legal_training/computer_forensics_training?src=ii

2. An excellent site for computer forensics-related resources:

   - http://www.forensics.nl/

ADDITIONAL READINGS

Below is a list of additional readings that may be useful in learning about the various aspects of digital forensics.

Carrier, B. (2005). *File System Forensic Analysis*. New York: Addison-Wesley Professional.

Casey, E. (2004). *Digital Evidence and Computer Crime*, 2nd ed. New York: Academic Press.

Craiger, P. (2006). Computer forensics methods and procedures. In H. Bigdoli (Ed.), *Handbook of Information Security*, Vol. 2. New York: John Wiley & Sons, pp. 715–749.

Craiger, P, Pollitt, M., and Swauger, J. (2006). Digital evidence and law enforcement. In H. Bigdoli (Ed.), *Handbook of Information Security*, Vol. 2. New York: John Wiley & Sons, pp. 679–701.

Jones, K.J., Bejtlich, R., and Rose, C.W. (2005). *Real Digital Forensics: Computer Security and Incident Response*. New York: Addison-Wesley Professional.

Kruse, W.G., II, and Heiser, J.G. (2002). *Computer Forensics: Incident Response Essentials*. New York: Addison-Wesley Professional.

Phillips, A., Nelson, B., Enfinger, F., and Steuart, C. (2005). *Guide to Computer Forensics and Investigations,* Second ed. New York: Course Technology.

Prosise, C., Mandia, K., and Pepe, M. (2005). *Incident Response and Computer Forensics*, Second ed. New York: McGraw-Hill Osborne.

REFERENCES

[1] Scientific Working Group on Digital Evidence. Available at www.swgde.org.

[2] Yasinsac, A., Earbacher, R., Marks, D.G., Pollitt, M., and Sommer, P.M. (2003). Computer forensics education. *IEEE Computer Security and Privacy Magazine* 1(4):15–23.

Chapter 3

Certification and Accreditation Overview

John J. Barbara

Summary

Certification and *accreditation* are different. Individuals become certified; laboratories attain accreditation. Both processes can be viewed as being indicative of the quality of services that are being offered. Certification provides the mechanism for an individual to demonstrate that he or she has attained a level of competence in a particular area. Attaining a specific certification credential usually requires satisfactorily completing oral tests, written test(s), and/or hands-on practical exercises.

Accreditation is a mechanism for a laboratory to demonstrate that its quality assurance system and its scientific practices are able to generate technically valid results. This is accomplished when external inspectors or assessors review all of the laboratory's operations (including its personnel, technical procedures, equipment, physical plant, security, and health and safety procedures) to determine compliance with established national and international standards and criteria. Whenever practical and applicable, the combination of certification(s) and accreditation compliment each other in the attainment of quality.

Key Words: Accreditation, ASCLD/LAB, Certification, CISCO, Computer forensics, GIAC, Information technology, SWGDE.

1. DETERMINING QUALITY PRACTICES

Certification and *accreditation* are two critical processes that are essential to ensuring quality practices and services. One of the overriding concerns or goals should be to attain "quality" and develop a means to measure or assess its effectiveness. *Quality assurance* is a means of assessing quality and includes both planned and systematic actions that management deems necessary to provide confidence that the product or service satisfies any specific requirements for quality. These actions may be the result

From: *Handbook of Digital and Multimedia Forensic Evidence*
Edited by: J. J. Barbara © Humana Press Inc., Totowa, NJ

of good scientific practice, best practices in the industry, regulatory requirements, or other controlling factors. A business that is providing technical consultant services pertaining to intrusion protection must be just as concerned about the overall quality of its practices as does a firearms examiner who identifies a projectile to a suspect weapon. Although quality is involved in both situations, the end result can be drastically different if quality measures are not in place. In the first instance, lack of specific technical knowledge (poor quality) could lead to a company's computer network being vulnerable to unauthorized access and the possible loss of intellectual data. This could be very costly in economic terms to the company. In the second instance, inaccurate or questionable analytical results (poor quality) may cause a suspect to be convicted of a homicide and, in some states, face the death penalty. Even though the end results are drastically different, there really should not be any difference in how management assesses the quality of its work product.

1.1. Individual Certification

When any business or entity seeks to hire a person, they usually consider the individual's educational background and his or her overall knowledge, skills, and abilities (KSAs). Most of us are aware that it is not always the most qualified individual that is hired to fill a particular vacancy. Available resources, including salary and benefits, often can be the controlling factors in determining who eventually is hired. Irrespective of resources, in the information technology (IT) industry, many individuals with preexisting certifications are very attractive to management:

> Corporations are dependent on cutting-edge computer and information technology to operate efficiently in an ever-competitive market driven economy. However, more often than not, these corporations lack the internal resources to effectively implement new technologies required to meet their needs. In these instances, they rely on information technology professionals to help implement technology driven solutions such as setting up a secure website or integrating their traditional brick and mortar business with Internet driven business models. They may also turn to IT professionals to help them manage the data management processes or automate their help-desk support systems *(1)*.

Once hired, the individual usually undergoes some sort of training regarding the software and hardware that he or she is expected to operate or oversee (severs, routers, etc.). Generally, the training will also include the practices of the business or organization. After the initial training has been completed, the individual then assumes his or her duties. In some instances, the business or organization self-certifies the individual when he or she has met certain standards, such as educational and training requirements, and has demonstrated a level of competence. However, certification should not be considered as a substitute for actual hands-on experience. Ideally, it is the combination of both experience and certification that provides an individual with the best all-around KSAs specific to the task. As is often the case, management may require employees to attain additional job-specific certification(s). From management's perspective, having certified staff serves as a means to demonstrate the quality of the product or service being offered. However, even though they require their staff to attain certification(s), certification itself is considered as an individual achievement. If the certified employee leaves the company, he or she leaves with his or her certification.

All of us are familiar with certification whether we realize it or not. When your vehicle is serviced at the car dealership, many (if not all) of the service technicians are "certified" to perform specific vehicle repairs. Not only does this provide the consumer with a degree of confidence, but also it is necessary for the automobile dealership to demonstrate that they offer quality services.

1.2. Accreditation Defined

Accreditation differs from certification in that it always pertains to the business or organization. It is part of an overall quality assurance program and can demonstrate that management practices and operations, personnel, procedures, the quality system, and the physical plant can meet or exceed certain national and/or international standards. Accreditation is usually considered as a voluntary process. However, if the services offered are of a forensic nature, then it is imperative that the entity become accredited. Several states have already passed legislation that requires any entity performing forensic analysis within that particular state to attain accreditation if the results of their analyses will be used in a court of law for prosecution purposes. Other states are considering similar legislation. Legislatures and the criminal justice system as a whole recognize the benefits of accreditation. Two of the essential standards and criteria that are indigenous to accreditation require that there be written, approved, standardized operational procedures and that the examiners undergo annual proficiency testing.

The combination of individual employees holding applicable certifications and accreditation (if applicable and available) can provide a means for the business or entity to demonstrate that its services are quality orientated. Although this is not any guarantee that errors or mistakes will not occur, an overall quality assurance program can and will lead to a better end product.

2. ATTAINING CERTIFICATION(S)

A person wishing to enter the field of IT is often faced with two fundamental questions: "What certifications should I obtain?" and "How and where do I go to get certified?" These questions are continually asked and are predicated upon the assumption that the individual has decided to pursue a chosen specific area in which to specialize. In researching these questions, it becomes obvious rather quickly that there really is not any one source to provide satisfactory answers to these questions. Neither is there any general consensus as to what certifications or industry-recognized credentials to attain for a specific area. Also, certification should be considered as a continual ongoing process and not a one-time event. Each certification attained increases the options and opportunities available to an individual and can be used as a foundation to enhance a chosen career path. There are a number of other fundamental issues that must also be addressed before pursuing certification(s).

All certifications are not equal and all do not require the same steps to be completed to obtain the certification. Becoming certified or attaining certification means that an individual completed the necessary steps outlined by the particular certification process. In some instances, an individual can become certified or attain certification by paying a fee or attending a 1- or 2-day training course or seminar. Other certifications require the individual to take written and/or practical tests. Still others require the successful completion of a series of training courses that may take several years. The attainment of a certification attests that the individual has successfully completed the requirements and can be expected to perform at a certain skill level. Certification generally provides (a) credibility to the individual by enhancing his or her confidence and skills level; (b) a means of recognizing personal achievement; and (c) a mechanism to ensure quality assurance. Many of the certifications available are recognized as industry standard credentials, and attaining one or more can improve the potential for job advancement and/or salary increases.

2.1. Certification Pathways

There are several steps to consider before proceeding with a certification or certification pathway. First, the individual has to assess the IT industry as a whole and decide his or her area of interest. Some of the services commonly found in the IT industry include systems management, disaster recovery, software and hardware installation, network administration, and information systems management. Irrespective of the area of interest, some issues need to be considered before proceeding:

1. **Choosing a certification (or certification pathway)**. Although this seems rather obvious, it can be very confusing to decide upon which certification(s) to choose or which pathway to pursue. Minimally, consider choosing one or two certifications that can serve as a stepping stone to a certification pathway. The decision should account for the area of interest (such as Network Administration or Wireless Local Area Network).
2. **What is the individual's experience level and how does it meet the requirements of the certification?** Some certifications require a minimum educational level and practical experience. If the individual cannot meet these requirements, then another certification needs to be considered or additional training has to be taken to attain the minimum requirements.
3. **Purchasing/reviewing appropriate study guides for the certification.** Consider purchasing appropriate study guides. Many include practice examination questions and can be found at local chain bookstores. Also, there are vendors that can provide hands-on training, either online or in a classroom environment or both.
4. **Signing up or registering to take the examination (if required) when the necessary knowledge and experience has been attained.** Depending upon the certification requirements, preparing for an examination can be a lengthy process. An important factor to be considered is that there may be minimum waiting periods before taking an examination as some may require the candidates to have a certain amount of experience. Also, if the person is unsuccessful in initially passing the testing requirements, there may be additional waiting periods before reapplying to take the test.
5. **Maintain the certification.** Again, this should be rather obvious. Most certifications generally require periodic retaking of an examination to be recertified. This may be necessary particularly if pursuing a certification pathway. Other certifications have no expiration date. The requirements (or none) for recertification should be considered as it will usually involve additional costs.

A listing of some currently available certifications for both IT professionals and for forensic analysis is included in this chapter. The listing is intended to provide basic knowledge and understanding of what credentials are available for those individuals interested in attaining certification. Time frames for completing the requirements for any given certification and the associated costs are not included in this listing. This is because different vendors may require varying amounts of time to complete the training and may charge different fees for their training or services.

IT certifications can be grouped into at least two different categories: Vendor and/or Product Specific and Vendor Neutral. For our purposes, Vendor and/or Product Specific IT certifications or applications are grouped (obviously) by vendor and include a brief description or definition describing what is covered by the certification. This allows for a better understanding of the different IT certification paths or pathways that could be attained and identifies the relationship between certain IT certifications. The Vendor Neutral IT certifications are listed alphabetically and also include a brief description or definition describing what is covered by the IT certification. Bear in mind that the listed IT certifications are not intended to imply that these are all of the certifications available or that any are being recommended. Rather, this should serve as a starting point or guide for those whose interest is in becoming certified.

Forensic analysis certifications also fall into two categories: Self Certification and Vendor Specific Certification. Currently, there are Vendor Specific Certifications for Computer Forensics and Video Analysis. These are discussed by type and category. It should be noted that many forensic training programs for Computer Forensics include requirements that the trainees successfully complete some of the Vendor Neutral IT certifications such as A+ and Network+. These Vendor Specific Certifications generally require a certain level of training and usually consist of two parts: an oral/written/online test and a hands-on practical test.

2.2. Vendor and/or Product Specific Certifications

2.2.1. CISCO Certifications

The number one leader in networking for the Internet is Cisco Systems, Inc. As all of us are aware, we cannot function without the infrastructure of our networks, and Cisco products, both software and hardware, are the foundation for most of those networks. Cisco has developed an extensive list of certifications that cover virtually all areas of internetworking for both the novice and the professional. Currently, they offer three different levels of certification: Associate, Professional, and Expert. Within these levels there are six different pathway choices, which would allow the individual to pick an appropriate certification pathway to meet the job requirements of a particular industry. Included among the pathways are Routing and Switching, Network Security, and Storage Networking. An individual can also pursue Qualified Specialist certifications pathways in eight additional areas, including those concerning Access Routing and LAN Switching, IP Communications, and Wireless LAN (2). Cisco Press publishes many specific guides and texts that can be purchased to serve as training tools in preparing for certification. Most large chain bookstores have them available or they can be ordered within a short period of time. Available Cisco certifications are listed alphabetically along with a brief description.

2.2.1.1. CISCO GENERAL CERTIFICATIONS

1. **CCNA (Cisco Certified Network Associate).** Intended for the professional who has attained the basic networking KSAs to install, configure, and operate small networks.

2. **CCDA (Cisco Certified Design Associate).** Intended for the professional who has attained the basic network KSAs to design routed and switched network infrastructures.

3. **CCNP (Cisco Certified Network Professional).** Intended for the professional who has advanced network KSAs and is able to install, configure, and troubleshoot medium-sized Local Area Networks (LANs) and Wide Area Networks (WANs).

4. **CCDP (Cisco Certified Design Professional).** Intended for the professional who has advanced knowledge of network design and is able to design routed and switched LANs, WANs, and dial access services.

5. **CCSP (Cisco Certified Security Professional).** Intended for the professional who has the necessary advanced KSAs to secure Cisco networks.

6. **CCIP (Cisco Certified Internetwork Professional).** Intended for the professional who has a detailed understanding of networking technologies and attained competency in infrastructure Internet Protocol (IP) networking solutions.

7. **CCVP (Cisco Certified Voice Professional).** Intended to provide and/or validate the professional skills that are necessary to integrate voice technology into existing network architectures.

8. **CCIE (Cisco Certified Internetwork Expert).** Certifications can be attained in several areas:

   A. **CCIE Routing & Switching.** Demonstrates an expert knowledge of networks, routers and switches.

   B. **CCIE Security.** Demonstrates an expert knowledge of specific security protocols and components.

   C. **CCIE Service Provider.** Demonstrates an expert knowledge and skills in the fundamentals of IP and core IP technologies.

   D. **CCIE Storage Networking.** Demonstrates expert knowledge of intelligent storage solutions over extended networks using options such as Fiber Channel and others.

   E. **CCIE Voice.** Demonstrates expert knowledge of Voice-over-IP (VoIP).

2.2.1.2. CISCO SPECIALIST CERTIFICATIONS

1. **Cisco Access Routing and LAN Switching Sales Specialist.** Intended for the professional who has the necessary functional knowledge to sell Cisco products.

2. **Cisco Access Routing and LAN Switching Specialist.** Intended for the professional who has the KSAs needed to implement and support complex networks.

3. **Cisco Routing and Switching Field Specialist.** Intended for the professional who has the KSAs to install, configure, monitor, and support Cisco products and solutions.

4. **Cisco Routing and Switching Sales Specialist.** Intended for the professional who has an understanding of routing and switching concepts that is necessary to sell end-to-end Cisco products and solutions.

5. **Cisco Routing and Switching Solutions Specialist.** Intended for the professional who has the KSAs to identify the individual requirements of customers and to create an applicable network solution using Cisco products and solutions.

6. **Cisco Content Networking.** Intended for the professional who has the necessary KSAs to plan, design, implement, and operate a Cisco Content Network (CN) solution.

7. **Cisco Foundation Express Design Specialist.** Intended for the professional who has a fundamental understanding of networks and routing and switching concepts. This would include the knowledge to incorporate wireless and security technologies in networks.

8. **Cisco Foundation Express Field Specialist.** Intended for the professional who has the KSAs to install, configure, operate, and support converged networks.
9. **Cisco Foundation Express Sales Specialist.** Intended for the professional who has the KSAs to sell converged network solutions.
10. **Cisco Advanced IP Communications Sales Specialist.** Intended for the professional who has the necessary KSAs to assess, recommend, and guide implementation of IP solutions for specific customer needs with emphasis on voice solutions.
11. **Cisco IP Communications Express Specialist.** Intended for the professional who has the fundamental VoIP technology skills necessary to install and maintain multiservice network solutions.
12. **Cisco IP Communications Express Sales Specialist.** Intended for the professional who has an understanding of IP communications solutions and who can demonstrate the KSAs to assess, recommend, and implement basic IP communications solutions.
13. **Cisco IP Contact Center Express Specialist.** Intended for the professional who has the KSAs necessary to plan, design, implement, and operate the Cisco IP Contact Center (IPCC) Express Edition.
14. **Cisco IP Telephony Design Specialist.** Intended for the professional who has the KSAs necessary to design IP Telephony multiservice network solutions.
15. **Cisco IP Telephony Operations Specialist.** Intended for the professional who has the KSAs necessary to operate and maintain IP Telephony multiservice network solutions.
16. **Cisco IP Telephony Support Specialist.** Intended for the professional who has the KSAs necessary to install and support IP Telephony multiservice network solutions.
17. **Cisco Rich Media Communications Specialist.** Intended for the professional who has the KSAs to design, implement, and support integrated voice, video, and Web collaboration in a converged network.
18. **Cisco Unity Design Specialist.** Intended for the professional who has the KSAs necessary to design and create Cisco Unity 4.0 solutions for customers.
19. **Cisco Unity Support Specialist.** Intended for the professional who has the KSAs necessary to install, configure, operate, and maintain a Cisco Unity 4.0 system (stand-alone voice mail and unified messaging environments).
20. **Cisco Optical Specialist.** Intended for the professional who has the KSAs necessary to design, install, operate, and maintain optical networking systems.
21. **Cisco Storage Networking Design Specialist.** Intended for the professional who has the KSAs necessary to design storage networking solutions based on converged architecture.
22. **Cisco Storage Networking Support Specialist.** Intended for the professional who has the KSAs necessary for installing, configuring, and maintaining Cisco storage products.
23. **Cisco Storage Networking Sales Specialist.** Intended for the professional who has knowledge of storage networking architecture (emphasis on the MDS 9000 product and its use in a SAN environment).
24. **Cisco Advanced Security Field Specialist.** Intended for the professional who has the KSAs necessary to install, configure, operate, and troubleshoot Network Admission Control (NAC), Cisco Security Monitoring Analysis and Response System (CS-MARS), and to identify, manage, and counter threats to secure networks.
25. **Cisco Firewall Specialist.** Intended for the professional who has the KSAs necessary to secure network access using Cisco IOS Software and Cisco PIX and Adaptive Security Appliance (ASA) Firewall Technologies.

26. **Cisco IPS Specialist.** Intended for the professional who has the KSAs to operate and monitor Cisco IOS Software and Intrusion Prevention Systems (IPS) technologies, which are used to prevent, understand, and respond to intrusion attempts.
27. **Cisco Security Sales Specialist.** Intended for the professional who has the KSAs necessary to sell components of the Cisco Self-Defending Network (SDN) strategy.
28. **Cisco Security Solutions and Design Specialist.** Intended for the professional who has knowledge of the Cisco Self-Defending Network strategy and the ability to design and sell Cisco Self-Defending Networks to customers.
29. **Cisco VPN Specialist.** Intended for the professional who has the KSAs necessary to configure Virtual Private Networks (VPNs) across shared public networks.
30. **Cisco VPN/Security Sales Specialist.** Intended for the professional who has the knowledge necessary to sell Cisco Virtual Private Network & Security solutions.
31. **Cisco Advanced Wireless LAN Sales Specialist.** Intended for the professional who has the knowledge necessary to sell Cisco wireless solutions and services.
32. **Cisco Wireless LAN Design Specialist.** Intended for the professional who has the KSAs necessary to design a wireless LAN associated with WLAN 802.11g standards.
33. **Cisco Wireless LAN Sales Specialist.** Intended for the professional who has the knowledge necessary to understand Cisco Wireless LAN concepts, systems, and applications in order to sell Cisco Wireless LAN solutions.
34. **Cisco Wireless LAN Support Specialist.** Intended for the professional who has the KSAs necessary to install, support, and operate a wireless LAN.

2.2.2. Citrix Certifications

Citrix is an enterprise software company whose focus is to simplify information and on-demand access for IT teams, users, and businesses. Citrix products are integrated to seamlessly provide secure, on-demand access to any business information resource from anywhere, with any device, over any network *(3)*.

1. **CCA (Citrix Certified Administrator).** Intended for the professional who has the basic KSAs necessary to support an existing implementation of Citrix Access Suite.
2. **CCEA (Citrix Certified Enterprise Administrator).** Intended for the professional who has the KSAs necessary to administer, build, test, roll out, and support multiple Citrix products.
3. **CCIA (Citrix Certified Integration Architect).** Intended for the professional that has acquired the knowledge, expertise, and credibility required for successful Citrix deployments.
4. **CCSP (Citrix Certified Sales Professional).** Intended for the professional who sells Citrix products and services as an access infrastructure solution.
5. **CCI (Citrix Certified Instructor).** Intended for the professional who will teach Citrix courseware.

2.2.3. CIW Certifications

These certifications are designed both for the individual entering the IT industry and for experienced IT professionals to expand their IT skills. CIW "spans various IT disciplines—including Web site design, enterprise development, network administration and security—as well as cross-functional areas that combine other disciplines, such as Web site management and Web development" *(4)*.

1. **CIW Associate.** Intended for professionals to demonstrate basic skills and knowledge of Internet technologies, network infrastructure, and Web authoring using HTML.
2. **CIW Professional.** Professionals holding the CIW Associate certification can attain this certification by passing at least one of eight CIW job-role exams in such areas as Web site design, security, server administration, and others.
3. **CIW Security Analyst.** For professionals holding a Master CIW Administrator certification, this certification provides the KSAs necessary to protect an organization's assets and operations.
4. **CIW Web Developer.** Intended for the professional who has the KSAs required to assemble and maintain Java^{TM}-based Web applications.
5. **Master CIW Administrator.** Intended for professionals whose career path is in network, system, or intranet administration.
6. **Master CIW Designer.** Intended for professionals who develop and maintain Web sites using authoring and scripting languages.
7. **Master CIW Enterprise Developer.** Intended for the professional who has the KSAs to develop enterprise-wide Web-enabled applications and implement complex e-business solutions.
8. **Master CIW Web Site Manager.** Intended for the professional who has the cross-functional set of Web skills necessary to act as a Web manager (networking, Web site design, Web authoring and scripting languages, and server administration).

2.2.4. CompTIA Certifications

For many years, the Computing Technology Industry Association (CompTIA) has been advancing the growth of the IT industry through standards, professional competence, and education and business solutions. CompTIA has developed specialized programs dedicated to major areas within the IT industry, one of the primary ones being training/certification for IT professionals. Certifications can be attained for A+, CDIA+, i-Net+, Network+, Server+, and Security+ *(5)*. These are described under Section 2.3.

2.2.5. GIAC (Global Information Assurance Certification)

See Section 2.2.13.

2.2.6. (ISC)²® Certifications

These certifications are offered under the auspices of the International Information Systems Security Certification Consortium (ISC)²®. They focus on educating and certifying information security professionals throughout his or her careers. Certifications include the Certified Information Systems Security Professional (CISSP®), CISSP Information Systems Security Engineering Professional (CISSP®-ISSEP®), Information Systems Security Architecture Professional (ISSAP®), Information Systems Security Management Professional (ISSMP®), Information Systems Security Engineering Professional (ISSEP®), the Certification and Accreditation Professional (CAP^{CM}), and the Systems Security Certified Practitioner (SSCP®). These are described under Section 2.3.

In April 2006, the American National Standards Institute (ANSI) granted accreditation to the CISSP Information Systems Security Engineering Professional

(CISSP®-ISSEP®) credential. This accreditation uses the ANSI/International Organization for Standardization/International Electrotechnical Commission 17024 standard. This standard, ANSI/ISO/IEC 17024, *General Requirements for Bodies Operating Certification of Persons,* facilitates accreditation by national bodies and is a benchmark for certification bodies offering certification of persons in any occupation.

2.2.7. Learning Tree International Certifications

Learning Tree International offers a wide range of certifications in the areas of IT and management. These certifications are designed to bridge the gap between an academic education and the necessary technical and management competencies needed by industry. Currently, there are 43 job-specific certification programs available in 13 different areas *(6).* Three of the areas, Windows Server 2003, SQL Server, and Exchange and Security, are summarized below.

2.2.7.1. WINDOWS SERVER 2003

1. **Windows Server 2003 Certified Professional.** Intended for the professional who has the KSAs and hands-on experience necessary to evaluate, design, and maintain a Windows Server 2003 environment.
2. **Windows Server 2003 Security Certified Professional.** Intended for the professional who has the KSAs to implement security on local and network resources in the Windows Server 2003 environment.
3. **Windows OS Advanced Administration Certified Professional.** Intended for the professional who has the KSAs to maintain, optimize and troubleshoot the Windows operating system environment.

2.2.7.2. SQL SERVER AND EXCHANGE PROFESSIONAL CERTIFICATION PROGRAMS

1. **SQL Server 2005 DBA Certified Professional.** Intended for the professional who has the KSAs to create and manage databases, implement security, and administer SQL Server 2005 with SQL Server Management Studio and Transact-SQL.
2. **SQL Server 2000 DBA Certified Professional.** Intended for the professional who has the KSAs to successfully administer and troubleshoot a large-scale SQL Server system within a Windows Server 2003 environment.
3. **SQL Server Application Development Certified Professional.** Intended for the professional who has the KSAs needed to create stored procedures and triggers and develop SQL queries that take full advantage of SQL Server's powerful facilities.
4. **Exchange Certified Professional.** Intended for the professional who has the KSAs to maintain the advanced messaging infrastructure provided by Exchange Server 2003 and minimize the impact of server disasters.

2.2.7.3. SECURITY

1. **Network Security Certified Professional.** Intended for the professional who has the KSAs to install and configure firewalls, to evaluate, implement, and manage secure remote access technologies, and to deploy a variety of intrusion detection systems.
2. **Enterprise and Web Security Certified Professional.** Intended for the professional who has the KSAs critical to maintaining the security of enterprise-level Web applications.

2.2.8. Microsoft Certifications

As a technology leader, Microsoft has developed a series of certifications that are designed to prepare and support the IT professional. The focus, obviously, is on Microsoft specific products. For those attaining one or more of these certifications, it is a means to demonstrate the KSAs that have been gained through training and experience.

1. **MCAD (Microsoft Certified Application Developer for Microsoft .NET).** Intended for the professional who has the KSAs to design, develop, and maintain department-level applications, components, Web or desktop clients, or back-end data services.

2. **MCDBA (Microsoft Certified Database Administrator on Microsoft SQL Server 2000).** Intended for the professional who has the KSAs to implement and administer Microsoft SQL Server™ databases.

3. **MCP (Microsoft Certified Professional).** Intended for the professional who has the KSAs to implement Microsoft products and/or technology as part of a business solution in an organization.

4. **MCSA (Microsoft Certified Systems Administrator).**

   A. **MCSA on Microsoft Windows 2000.** Intended for the professional who has the KSAs to successfully manage and troubleshoot system environments running on the Windows 2000 operating system and Windows .NET Server platforms.

   B. **MCSA on Microsoft Windows Server 2003.** Intended for the professional who has the KSAs to successfully manage and maintain the complex computing environment of medium- to large-sized companies operating on the Microsoft Windows Server 2003 System.

5. **MCSD (Microsoft Certified Solution Developer for Microsoft .NET).** Intended for the lead developer professional who has the KSAs to design and develop leading-edge enterprise solutions with Microsoft development tools, technologies, platforms, and the Microsoft .NET Framework.

6. **MCSE (Microsoft Certified Systems Engineer).** This is probably one of the most sought-after certifications in the IT industry. Attaining certification demonstrates the professional's expertise in designing and implementing the infrastructure for business solutions based on the Microsoft Windows 2000 platform and Microsoft Windows Server System.

7. **MOS (Microsoft Office Specialist).** Intended for the professional who has the KSAs to demonstrate technical proficiency and expertise in the use of Microsoft Office and other software desktop applications. There are different certification tracks for Microsoft Office Suites 97, 2000, and XP.

2.2.9. Novell Certifications

Novell is one of the world's leading companies providing enterprise class software and services. Historically, they have been a leader in the open source movement. As a Linux software company, they provide total support for the entire Linux environment. Novell certifications were among the first offered in the IT industry and they established the standard for IT certifications *(7)*.

1. **CNA (Certified Novel Administrator).** Intended for the professional who has the KSAs to support Novell NetWare and eDirectory environments.

2. **CNE (Certified Novel Engineer).** Intended for the professional who has the KSAs to support a network. This includes planning, configuring, installing, upgrading, and troubleshooting Novell NetWare and eDirectory environments.

3. **MCNE (Master Certified Novel Engineer).** Intended for the CNE professional who has the additional specialized training necessary to perform implementation and troubleshooting on specific types of Novell systems.

4. **CNI (Certified Novell Instructor).** Intended for the professional who has the KSAs to become a Novell instructor who teaches the official Novell curriculum.
5. **NAI (Novell Academic Instructor).** Intended for the professional who has the KSAs to teach certified courses at authorized Novell Academic Training Partner or Novell Technical Institute locations.
6. **CNS (Certified Novell Salesperson).** Intended for the professional who has the KSAs to competently explain, demonstrate, and sell Novell products and solutions.
7. **NCLE (Novell Certified Linux Engineer).** Intended for the professional who has the KSAs to administer and install Linux-based Novell Enterprise services in both mixed and exclusively Linux-based environments.
8. **Novell Certified Linux Engineer 9.** Intended for the professional who has the KSAs to master advanced SUSE Linux Enterprise Server administration.
9. **NCLP (Novell Certified Linux Professional).** Intended for the professional who has the KSAs to install Linux servers into a network environment and manage users and groups. This also would include troubleshooting, managing, and compiling the Linux kernel.

2.2.10. Oracle Certifications

The Oracle Corporation is recognized as the industry leader in offering infrastructure software for databases, middleware, and for enterprise management. They were the first to introduce Relational Database Management Systems (RDBMS) using IBM's Structured Query Language (SQL) technology. Today, they are the world's largest RDBMS vendor. Oracle offers several certification pathways. These are highly sought-after, industry-recognized credentials for IT professionals. The pathways include Oracle 9i Database, Oracle 9i Application Server, Oracle Database 10g, Oracle Application Server 10g, Oracle Application Developer, and Oracle Internet Application Developer *(8)*.

2.2.10.1. ORACLE 9I DATABASE

1. **Oracle9i Database Administrator Certified Associate.** Intended for the professional who has attained the basic foundational KSAs necessary to administer The Oracle 9i Database.
2. **Oracle9i Database Administrator Certified Professional.** Intended for the professional who has the KSAs to manage database functions including network administration, backup and recovery, and tuning an Oracle 9i Database.
3. **Oracle9i Database Administrator Certified Master.** Intended for the professional who has attained comprehensive and extensive KSAs in the areas of installing, troubleshooting, backup and recovery, and tuning of the Oracle 9i Database.

2.2.10.2. ORACLE 9I APPLICATION SERVER

1. **Oracle Application Server 9i Web Administrator Certified Associate.** Intended for the professional who has the KSAs to administer, monitor, and secure an Oracle9iAS environment.

2.2.10.3. ORACLE DATABASE 10G

1. **Oracle Database 10g Administrator Certified Associate.** Intended for the professional who has the basic foundational KSAs necessary to administer the Oracle Database 10g.

2. **Oracle Database 10g Administrator Certified Professional.** Intended for the professional who has the KSAs to configure an Oracle database for multilingual applications and to use various methods of recovering and tuning databases using Oracle technologies.
3. **Oracle Database 10g Administrator Certified Master.** Intended for the professional who has attained comprehensive KSAs in the areas of installing, troubleshooting, backup and recovery, and tuning of Oracle Database 10g.

2.2.10.4. ORACLE APPLICATION SERVER 10G

1. **Oracle Application Server 10g Administrator.** Certified Associate: Intended for the professional who has attained the basic KSAs necessary to access and use Oracle Application Server 10g management tools and perform basic management tasks.
2. **Oracle Application Server 10g Administrator.** Certified Professional: Intended for the professional who has advanced KSAs to effectively install and manage nondefault Oracle Application Server 10g installations.

2.2.10.5. ORACLE APPLICATION DEVELOPER

1. **Oracle PL/SQL Developer Certified Associate.** Intended for the professional who has attained the KSAs to use PL/SQL programming language to build Internet applications for both Oracle9i and Oracle Database 10g.
2. **Oracle Forms Developer Certified Professional.** Intended for the professional who can demonstrate proficiency and competency with Oracle development tools and has the KSAs required to build Internet applications.

2.2.10.6. ORACLE INTERNET APPLICATION DEVELOPER

1. **Oracle Internet Application Developer Rel. 6i Certified Professional.** Intended for the professional who has the KSAs to develop and deploy Internet applications in a development environment using Oracle Forms.

2.2.11. Red Hat Certifications

Red Hat was founded in 1993 and is considered the leader in Linux and open source solutions. Based on their Red Hat Enterprise Linux technology, they provide operating system platforms and applications along with management solutions, support, training, and consulting services. Certifications can be attained in four primary areas *(9)*.

1. **RHCE (Red Hat Certified Engineer).** Intended for the professional who has attained the KSAs necessary to set up and manage Red Hat or UNIX servers running production network services and security.
2. **RHCT (Red Hat Certified Technician).** Intended for the professional who has attained the KSAs necessary to install, configure, and attach Red Hat Linux systems to a corporate network.
3. **RHCA (Red Hat Certified Architect).** Intended for the professional RHCE Linux system administrator who has the KSAs to plan, design, and manage open source infrastructure in large enterprise environments.
4. **RHCSS (Red Hat Certified Security Specialist).** Intended for the professional who has attained the advanced KSAs using Red Hat Enterprise Linux, SELinux, and Red Hat Directory Server.

2.2.12. RSA Certifications

RSA Security Professional Services organization offers a full range of services to assist with the deployment and enhancement of industry technological investments. Services include meeting business needs in securing new technologies, expanding use of the Internet, securing an Intranet, satisfying regulatory requirements, supporting product upgrades, and integrating third-party applications. They also offer the RSA Certified Security Professional Program *(10)*.

1. **RSA SecurID Certified Systems Engineer.** Intended for the professional who has attained the KSAs necessary to provide technical support, sales support, and/or technical implementation of security systems working with the RSA SecurID product.
2. **RSA SecurID Administrator.** Intended for the professional who has attained the KSAs necessary to work in a Help Desk, Call Center, or manage an RSA SecurID system or RSA Authentication Manager (RSA ACE/Server) installation.
3. **RSA SecurID Certified Instructor.** Intended for the professional who has attained the KSAs necessary to teach individuals how to deploy and maintain enterprise security systems that use RSA SecurID products.
4. **RSA ClearTrust Certified Systems Engineer.** Intended for the professional who has attained the KSAs necessary to install and configure enterprise security systems that use RSA ClearTrust products.
5. **RSA Keon Certified Systems Engineer.** Intended for the professional who has attained the KSAs necessary to install and configure enterprise security systems that use RSA Keon products.

2.2.13. SANS Certifications

The SANS Institute was established in 1989 to be a research and education organization. In response to the needs of security professionals, the SANS Institute started the Global Information Assurance Certification (GIAC) program in 1999. Its intent was and is to provide professionals with an appropriate level of knowledge and skills regarding information security. Certifications and certificates are offered in many areas, including Intrusion Detection, Incident Handling, Forensics, and Windows and UNIX Operating System Security *(11)*. Certifications are based on successful completion of a full 5- or 6-day course. Certificates are based on successful completion of a 1- or 2-day course. Today, SANS (SysAdmin, Audit, Network, and Security) is probably the single largest source for information security training and certification in the world.

2.2.13.1. GIAC CERTIFICATIONS

1. **GIAC Information Security Fundamentals (GISF).** Intended for professionals such as Managers, Information Security Officers, and System Administrators who need an overview of information assurance, risk management, and defense in-depth techniques.
2. **GIAC Security Essentials Certification (GSEC).** Intended for security professionals who have the KSAs required to implement information security practices.
3. **GIAC Certified Firewall Analyst (GCFW).** Intended for the professional who has attained the KSAs necessary to design, configure, and monitor routers, firewalls, and perimeter defense systems.
4. **GIAC Certified Intrusion Analyst (GCIA).** Intended for the professional who has attained the KSAs necessary to configure and monitor intrusion detection systems and to read, interpret, and analyze network traffic and related log files.

5. **GIAC Certified Incident Handler (GCIH).** Intended for the professional who has attained the KSAs necessary to understand common attack techniques and tools and to defend against and/or respond to such attacks when they occur.

6. **GIAC Certified Windows Security Administrator (GCWN).** Intended for the professional who has attained the KSAs necessary to secure and audit Windows systems, including services such as Group Policy, Active Directory, Internet Information Server, IPSec and Certificate Services.

7. **GIAC Certified UNIX Security Administrator (GCUX).** Intended for the professional who has attained the KSAs necessary to secure and audit UNIX and Linux systems.

8. **GIAC Certified Forensics Analyst (GCFA).** Intended for the professional who has attained the KSAs necessary to handle advanced incident handling scenarios, conduct formal incident investigations, and carry out forensic investigation of networks and hosts.

9. **GIAC Assessing Wireless Networks (GAWN).** Intended for the professional who has attained the KSAs necessary to assess the security of wireless networks

10. **GIAC .Net (GNET).** Intended for the professional who has attained the KSAs necessary to securing .Net code or a Microsoft Web-based architecture.

11. **GIAS Secure Internet Presence (GSIP).** Intended for the professional who has attained the KSAs necessary to install, configure, develop, and monitor secure Web applications using Linux systems with Apache web server, MySQL databases, and the PHP scripting language (LAMP).

12. **GIAC Certified Security Consultant (GCSC).** Intended for the professional who has attained the KSAs necessary to manage the technical, business, and project management responsibilities related to security consultant practices.

13. **GIAC Security Leadership Certification (GSLC).** Intended for the professional who has attained the KSAs relating to current security issues, best practices, and technology.

14. **GIAC Security Audit Essentials (GSAE).** Intended for the professional who has attained the KSAs necessary to develop best practice audit checklists.

15. **GIAC Certified ISO-17799 Specialist (G7799).** Intended for the professional who has attained the KSAs necessary to understand the ISO 17799 security standard and the ability to put the standard into practice.

16. **GIAC Systems and Network Auditor (GSNA).** Intended for the professional who has attained the KSAs necessary to apply basic risk analysis techniques and to conduct a technical audit of essential information systems.

17. **GSM Platinum Certification.** Intended for the professional who completed three GIAC certifications (GCIH, GCFA, and GREM) and is aspiring to master all of the essential elements concerning malware.

18. **GSC Platinum Certification.** Intended for the professional who completed four GIAC certifications (G7799, GSNA, GPCI, and GSPA) and is pursuing in-depth technical knowledge in the area of compliance.

19. **GSE Certification.** Intended for the professional who completed three GIAC certifications (GSEC, GCIA, and GCIH) and is pursuing in-depth technical education in all areas of information security.

2.2.13.2. GIAC CERTIFICATES

1. **Stay Sharp Program - Mastering Packet Analysis (SSP-MPA).** Intended for the professional who has attained the KSAs necessary to understand. Transmission Control Protocols and Internet Protocols and to dissect packets to understand how they work.

2. **Securing Windows 2000 - The Gold Standard (GGSC-0100).** Intended for the professional who has attained the KSAs necessary to quickly and repeatable secure Windows 2000 Professional systems.

3. **Securing Solaris - The Gold Standard (GGSC-0200).** Intended for the professional who has attained the KSAs necessary to hardening Solaris 8 & 9 systems following the CIS benchmark.

4. **Auditing Cisco Routers - The Gold Standard (GGSC-0400).** Intended for the professional who has attained the KSAs necessary to assess and improve the security of Cisco routers.

5. **GIAC Cutting Edge Hacking Techniques (GHTQ).** Intended for the professional to attain knowledge of the latest tools and techniques used by hackers.

6. **GIAC Web Application Security (GWAS).** Intended for the professional who wishes to attain the knowledge necessary to implement secure Web application design.

7. **GIAC Intrusion Prevention (GIPS).** Intended for Firewall, Intrusion Detection System (IDS), and Intrusion Prevention Systems (IPS) administrators and network security staff who have attained the KSAs necessary to understand such topics as IPSs, IDSs, and firewalls and deep packet inspection.

8. **GIAC Reverse Engineering Malware (GREM).** Intended for the professional who has attained the KSAs necessary to protect an organization from malicious code.

9. **GIAC Fundamentals of Information Security Policy (GFSP).** Intended for the professional who has attained the KSAs necessary to creating and maintaining security policy and procedures.

10. **Ethics in IT (GEIT).** Intended for all IT professional's to provide an understanding of an IT professional's code of ethics.

11. **GIAC HIPAA Security Implementation (GHSC).** Intended for the professional who is responsible for information security at a health care–related operation. Professionals attain knowledge of the Health Insurance Portability and Accountability Act (HIPPA) security regulations and can demonstrate the ability to enforce the administrative, physical, and technical safeguards required by the HIPAA Security Rule.

12. **GIAC E-warfare (GEWF).** Intended for the professional who seeks knowledge regarding information warfare and its application to business.

13. **GIAC Critical Infrastructure Protection (GCIP).** Intended to provide knowledge concerning critical infrastructure protection to professionals such as Security Officers, Risk Managers, and Incident Handlers.

14. **GIAC Security Policy and Awareness (GSPA).** Intended for professionals who write, implement, or are responsible for security awareness programs.

15. **GIAC Operations Essentials Certification (GOEC).** Intended for the professional who has attained the KSAs necessary to be a productive member of operations and system administration teams.

16. **GIAC Business Law and Computer Security (GBLC).** Intended for the professional to attain an understanding of the issues concerning information security management and legal/regulatory considerations.

17. **GIAC Contracting for Data Security (GCDS).** Intended for the nonattorney professional to provide familiarization with contracts that may contain data security provisions.

18. **GIAC Law of Fraud (GLFR).** Intended for the nonattorney professional to provide familiarization with the requirements of the Sarbanes-Oxley Act and other laws related to financial reporting and white collar crime.

19. **GIAC Legal Issues in Information Technologies (GLIT).** Intended for the nonattorney professional to provide the knowledge and ability to write better security policies.
20. **GIAC Payment Card Industry (GPCI).** Intended for the professional to provide the KSAs necessary to operate in a PCI CISP compliant environment.

2.2.14. Sun Certifications

Sun Microsystems, Inc., was founded in 1982 and manufactures computers, computer components, software, and information-technology services. They were an early advocate of UNIX-based networked computing and their products include servers, workstations, the Solaris Operating System, the Network File System, and the Java platform. Sun offers four certification pathways: Java Technology, Solaris Operating System, Directory Server, and Custom Certification *(12)*.

2.2.14.1. JAVA TECHNOLOGY

1. **Sun Certified Associate for the Java 2 Platform (SCJA).** Intended for the entry level professional Java programmer pursing an application development or software project management career using the Java 2 Platform, Standard Edition (J2SE) technology.
2. **Sun Certified Programmer for the Java 2 Platform (SCJP).** Intended for the professional Java programmer to demonstrate proficiency in the fundamentals of Java programming using the Java 2 Platform, Standard Edition (J2SE) technology.
3. **Sun Certified Developer for the Java 2 Platform (SCJD).** Intended for the professional Sun Certified Programmer to demonstrate his or her advanced proficiency in developing production-level applications using Java 2 Platform, Standard Edition (J2SE) technology.
4. **Sun Certified Business Component Developer for the Java 2 Platform (SCBCD).** Intended for the professional Sun Certified Programmer who specializes in Java 2 Platform and/or Enterprise Edition (J2EE) platform technologies that are used to develop server-side components that encapsulate the business logic of an application.
5. **Sun Certified Web Component Developer for the Java 2 Platform (SCWCD).** Intended for the professional Sun Certified Programmer who specializes in the application of JavaServer Pages and servlet technologies using Java 2 Platform, Enterprise Edition (J2EE) platform.
6. **Sun Certified Developer for Java Web Services (SCDJWS).** Intended for the professional Sun Certified Programmer who creates Web services applications using Java technology components.
7. **Sun Certified Mobile Application Developer for the Java 2 Platform, Micro Edition (SMAD).** Intended for the professional Sun Certified Programmer who creates mobile applications for cell phones or "smart" devices using the Java 2 Platform, Mobile Edition (J2ME) platform.
8. **Sun Certified Enterprise Architect for the Java 2 Platform, Enterprise Edition (SCEA).** Intended for the professional who is responsible for architecting and designing Java 2 Platform, Enterprise Edition (J2EE) technology compliant applications.

2.2.14.2. SOLARIS OPERATING SYSTEM

1. **Sun Certified System Administration for the Solaris Operating System.** Intended for the professional who has attained the KSAs necessary to perform essential system administration procedures and administer a networked server running on the Solaris Operating System.

2. **Sun Certified Network Administration for the Solaris Operating System.** Intended for the experienced System Administrator professional who has attained the KSAs necessary to administering Sun systems in a networked environment that includes LANs and the Solaris Operating System.

3. **Sun Certified Security Administration for the Solaris Operating System.** Intended for the experienced Security Administration professional who is responsible for administering security in a Solaris Operating System.

2.2.14.3. DIRECTORY SERVER

1. **Sun Certified Engineer for Sun One Directory Server 5.x.** Intended for the professional who has attained the KSAs necessary to design, deploy, configure, administer, and troubleshoot the Sun ONE Directory Server 5.x for enterprise-level solutions.

2.2.14.4. CUSTOM CERTIFICATIONS

Sun can assist companies who employ technologies for which the IT industry does not offer certifications. After thoroughly gathering data, consultants can design and deliver certification testing to the companies.

2.2.15. Symantec Certifications

Symantec Corporation is the world leader in Internet security. Founded in 1982, Symantec employs thousands of engineers to design and develop solutions to help individuals and business secure their information. They are the providers of many widely used products such as Norton AntiVirus, Norton Internet Security, Norton SystemWorks, and Norton Personal Firewall. Symantec offers certification credentials at three different levels *(13)*.

1. **Symantec Certified Technology Architects (SCTA).** Intended for the professional who has attained the KSAs necessary to design, plan, deploy, and manage effective security solutions.

2. **Symantec Certified Security Engineers (SCSE).** Intended for the professional who has attained the KSAs to provide implementation and management of solutions in a particular security segment.

3. **Symantec Certified Security Practitioners (SCSP).** Intended for the professional who has attained the KSAs to become a senior security consultant who has an in-depth knowledge and expertise concerning multiple security segments.

2.2.16. The Security Certified Program Certifications

There are two certifications offered under The Security Certified Program (The SCP).

1. **SCNA (Security Certified Network Architect).** Intended for the professional who has attained the KSAs necessary to build trusted networks.

2. **SCNP (Security Certified Network Professional).** Intended for the professional who has attained the KSAs necessary for understanding defensive security strategies.

2.3. Vendor Neutral IT Certifications

1. **A+.** This is a two-part certification process that covers both hardware and operating systems. The hardware examination is designed to demonstrate knowledge of micro-computer systems (installation, configuration, upgrading, and troubleshooting). The operating system examination is designed to demonstrate an individual's knowledge

of the command line and for installing, configuring, upgrading, and troubleshooting operating systems. (Note: Many Computer Forensic training programs require A+ certification).

2. **CDIA+ (Certified Document Imaging Architect).** Allows individuals to demonstrate competency and professionalism in all major areas and technologies used to plan, design, and specify an imaging system.

3. **CISSP® (Certified Information Systems Security Professional).** This was the first ANSI ISO accredited certification in the field of information security. It provides an objective measure of competence in the 10 domains of the (ISC)² CISSP® CBK®.

4. **CISSP®-ISSEP® (CISSP Information Systems Security Engineering Professional).** This credential was established several years ago as a cooperative effort between (ISC)²® and the National Security Administration (NSA). It is intended for professionals who can demonstrate that they have attained an additional level of KSAs unique to U.S. national security employees and contractors.

5. **CAP^CM (Certification and Accreditation Professional).** Intended to provide professionals with the KSAs required for those involved in the certification and accreditation process.

6. **i-Net+.** This certification is intended for entry-level technical professionals who would be responsible for maintaining Internet, intranet, and extranet infrastructure and services as well as the development of Web-related applications.

7. **ISSAP® (Information Systems Security Architecture Professional).** Intended for CISSPs to demonstrate competence in the requirements for information security architecture.

8. **ISSEP® (Information Systems Security Engineering Professional).** Intended for CISSPs to demonstrate competence in the requirements for information security engineering.

9. **ISSMP® (Information Systems Security Management Professional).** Intended for CISSPs to demonstrate competence in the requirements for information security management.

10. **Linux+.** Intended to demonstrate the knowledge and skills (competency) of Linux system administrators with at least 6 months practical experience.

11. **Network+.** Intended for network technicians with at least 18 months experience to demonstrate knowledge of configuration and installation of the TCP/IP client.

12. **Project+.** Intended for IT professionals to demonstrate competency in the business knowledge, interpersonal skills, and project management processes required to successfully manage IT projects.

13. **Security+.** Covers topics such as access control, intrusion detection, malicious code, cryptography, physical security, and others and is intended to demonstrate IT security skills.

14. **Server+.** Intended for individuals with at least 18 months of IT experience with server installation, troubleshooting, and support. The examination covers network hardware such as Small Computer System Interface (SCSI), Redundant Array of Independent Drives (RAID), and Storage Area Network Systems (SANS).

15. **SSCP® (Systems Security Certified Practitioner).** Intended for information security practitioners to demonstrate their level of competence with the seven domains of the compendium of best practices for information security, the (ISC)² SSCP CBK®.

2.4. *Forensic Analysis Certifications*

1. **AccessData Certified Examiner (ACE)** *(14)*. This credential is intended for both the private and public sector professional forensic examiner who can demonstrate his

or her proficiency in the use of the Forensic Toolkit (FTK), the FTK Imager, the Password Recovery Toolkit, and the Registry Viewer (all AccessData products).

2. **Certified Computer Examiner (CCE)** *(15)*. This credential is offered by the International Society of Computer Forensic Examiners (ISCFE) to both law enforcement and non–law enforcement forensic computer examiners. ISCFE is a private Florida corporation affiliated with Key Computer Service, Inc. Candidates wishing to attain this credential cannot have a prior criminal record and must have the appropriate computer forensics training and experience.

3. **Forensic Video Analyst Certification Program** *(16)*. This program, offered by the Law Enforcement & Emergency Services Video Association (LEVA), is currently the only forensic video certification program in the United States. LEVA is a nonprofit organization committed to improving the quality of video training and promoting the use of state-of-the-art, effective equipment in the law enforcement and emergency services community. This certification credential has been offered since 2004.

4. **Guidance Software (EnCe)** *(17)*. This certification credential is intended for both the private and public sector professional forensic examiner who uses EnCase as his or her digital evidence/computer forensic software tool.

5. **High Tech Crime Institute and HTCI @ LC Technology** *(18)*. Offers such courses as "Forensic Processing of Digital Media," "Computer Crime Essentials," and others that can lead to a Computer Crime Scene Technician Certification (CCST). Once this certification has been obtained, there are other certification tracks that can be followed, including the Certified Computer Network Investigator (CCNI), the Certified Computer Forensic Technician (CCFT), and the Forensic Operating Systems Specialist (FOSS).

6. **IACIS Certified Forensic Computer Examiner (CFCE)** *(19)*. The International Association of Computer Investigative Specialists (IACIS) is a volunteer nonprofit corporation composed of federal, state, local, and international law enforcement professionals. They offer both on-site and external CFCE certification for qualified professional forensic examiners.

3. BRIEF HISTORICAL BACKGROUND LEADING TO THE DIGITAL & MULTIMEDIA EVIDENCE DISCIPLINE

The Scientific Working Group on Digital Evidence (SWGDE) was established in 1998 with the objective to bring together federal crime laboratory directors in the United States whose agencies were engaged in the analysis of digital media. SWGDE soon expanded to include representatives from state and local law enforcement agencies including the Illinois State Police Crime Laboratories, the North Carolina State Bureau of Investigation, and the Florida Department of Law Enforcement.

Shortly thereafter, it became apparent to SWGDE that examiners were conducting a wide diversity of digital and multimedia analyses. Typical analyses included computer analysis, digital optical media analysis, cellular telephone analysis, video analysis, digital camera analysis, image analysis, audio analysis, and others. In an effort to better delineate this diversity, the membership proposed creating a new discipline that would better define or characterize what was meant by "digital forensic analysis." Subsequently, this led to the creation of the Digital Evidence discipline, which was further defined to be composed of four subdisciplines: Computer Forensics, Forensic

Audio, Image Analysis, and Video Analysis. SWGDE then began to explore the possibility of having the new discipline become an accredited discipline within the American Society of Crime Laboratory Directors/Laboratory Accrediting Boards' (ASCLD/LABs) existing forensic laboratory accreditation program. In July 2003, the American Society of Crime Laboratory Directors (ASCLD) delegate assembly membership approved the addition of the Digital Evidence discipline (and its four subdisciplines) to the ASCLD/LAB Legacy accreditation program. ASCLD/LAB changed the discipline's name to the "Digital & Multimedia Evidence" discipline in 2005 as was requested by SWGDE. This was to allow agencies that were performing analog video analysis to be included in the accreditation process. Also at that time, the following definitions were added to the ASCLD/LAB Legacy Manual:

1. **Multimedia Evidence.** Analog or digital media, including, but not limited to film, tape, magnetic, and optical media, and/or the information contained therein.
2. **Computer Forensics.** A subdiscipline of Digital & Multimedia Evidence that involves the examination, analysis, and/or evaluation of digital evidence.
3. **Forensic Audio.** A subdiscipline of Digital & Multimedia Evidence that involves the examination, analysis, and/or evaluation of audio.
4. **Image Analysis.** A subdiscipline of Digital & Multimedia Evidence that involves the application of image science and domain expertise to examine and interpret the content of an image and/or the image itself.
5. **Video Analysis.** A subdiscipline of Digital & Multimedia Evidence that involves the examination, analysis, and/or evaluation of video *(20)*.

4. ASCLD/LAB Accreditation Programs

For forensic crime laboratories, ASCLD/LAB offers two voluntary accreditation programs: the ASCLD/LAB Legacy Program and the ASCLD/LAB-*International* Program. Accreditation can be obtained in the disciplines of Biology (DNA), Controlled Substances, Crime Scene, Digital & Multimedia Evidence, Firearms and Toolmarks, Latent Prints, Questioned Documents, Toxicology, and Trace Evidence. ASCLD/LAB's first accreditation program, now called the Legacy Program, began in 1982. The ASCLD delegate assembly membership approved the ASCLD/LAB-*International* Program in late 2003 and it became effective on April 1, 2004. Originally, this program combined the ISO/IEC 17025:1999 standards and the ASCLD/LAB-*International* Supplemental Requirements. ISO/IEC 17025:1999 is an internationally recognized standard that contains all of the requirements that testing and calibration laboratories have to meet if they wish to demonstrate that they operate a quality system, are technically competent, and are able to generate technically valid results. National and international accreditation bodies that recognize the competence of testing and calibration laboratories use the ISO/IEC 17025:1999 standard as the basis for accreditation. (Note: The current version is ISO/IEC 17025:2005). The Supplemental Requirements are based on the essential elements of the ASCLD/LAB Legacy Program and the ILAC G-19 standards. As of June 10, 2007, ASCLD/LAB had accredited 334 crime laboratories in the United States, Australia, Canada, Hong Kong, New Zealand, and Singapore. This included 182 state laboratories, 100 local agency laboratories, 22 federal laboratories, 10 international laboratories, and 20 private laboratories. Of the total, 298 are accredited under the Legacy Program and 36 are accredited under the *International* Program *(21)*.

4.1. Commonalities Between ASCLD/LAB's Accreditation Programs

Because both accreditation programs are voluntary, any forensic crime laboratory can apply for accreditation in either program (but not both). A laboratory can submit its application for accreditation when it determines that its management, operations, personnel, procedures, equipment, physical plant, security, and health and safety procedures can meet the established standards and criteria of the program selected. It is important to note that both programs accredit laboratories but neither certifies individual examiners in any of the forensic disciplines. Accreditation pertains to laboratories and certification pertains to individual examiners. After the laboratory has demonstrated that it can comply with applicable established standards and criteria, it may become ASCLD/LAB Legacy or ASCLD/LAB-*International* accredited. The individual examiners in both programs must comply with specific requirements in the areas of education, training, competency testing, and proficiency testing. As a result of this process, many ASCLD/LAB accredited laboratories self-certify their examiners in the individual ASCLD/LAB disciplines. Under these circumstances, self-certification validates the education, training, competency testing, and proficiency testing requirements that examiners must meet prior to performing independent casework analysis.

A forensic crime laboratory performing analysis in any or all of the aforementioned forensic disciplines (except Crime Scene) must seek accreditation for all those disciplines when applying for accreditation or re-accreditation. The laboratory must decide upon which accreditation program best serves its needs. It cannot apply for ASCLD/LAB Legacy accreditation in one discipline and ASCLD/LAB-*International* accreditation in another discipline. Specifically pertaining to the Digital & Multimedia Evidence discipline, any entity performing analysis in any of the four subdisciplines is considered by ASCLD/LAB as a laboratory.

4.2. Differences Between the Two Accreditation Programs

The current ASCLD/LAB Legacy Manual (2005 version as of this writing) consists of statements of principles, the basic standards, 151 criteria for evaluation of the standards, and discussions to provide more detailed explanations of the criteria. These are categorized into 90 Essential, 45 Important, and 16 Desirable criteria. Any stand-alone Digital & Multimedia Evidence section, unit, or laboratory applying for accreditation must demonstrate documented compliance with at least 108 of these criteria (50 essential, 42 important, and 16 desirable) before accreditation can be obtained. Additionally, there are nine more essential criteria applicable if the stand-alone section or unit utilizes technical support personnel (four essential) and/or has a crime scene function (five Essential). Accreditation is granted by the ASCLD/LAB Board once the laboratory attains compliance with 100% of the applicable essential criteria, 75% of the applicable important criteria, and 50% of the applicable desirable criteria. No other combination is acceptable. The laboratory is accredited for a 5-year accreditation cycle and remains accredited as long as it continues to comply with the standards and criteria that lead to its accreditation. An annual self-assessment is required that must be submitted to ASCLD/LAB.

To attain accreditation under the ASCLD/LAB-*International* program, a laboratory must demonstrate conformance to the applicable requirements of both the ISO/IEC 17025:2005 *General Requirements for the Competence of Testing and*

Calibration Laboratories and the ASCLD/LAB-*International* Supplemental Requirements for the Accreditation of Forensic Science Testing and Calibration Laboratories. Although there are at least 385 standards or clauses that are potentially applicable, for a Digital & Multimedia Evidence section or unit the number is considerably less since standards or clauses that pertain to calibration are generally not applicable. However, all applicable standard or clauses must be scored as "Yes" for a laboratory to attain accreditation. This is a major difference between the two programs. Also the *International* Program's 5-year accreditation cycle requires an annual surveillance visit. The laboratory will receive advance notice of the surveillance visit and which accreditation requirements will be reviewed.

5. CONCLUSION

Individual certification(s) and laboratory accreditation are processes that can help define quality. Individual certification(s) are just that, for the individual to demonstrate that he or she has attained a level of competence in a particular area. Likewise, attaining accreditation demonstrates that a laboratory and its practices have achieved a recognized level of competence in the services that it offers. The combination of individual certification(s) and laboratory accreditation (when applicable and available) compliment each other in the attainment of quality.

REFERENCES

[1] Available at http://www.compucert.com/information-technology.html.

[2] Available at http://www.cisco.com.

[3] Available at http://www.citrix.com.

[4] Available at http://www.ciwcertified.com/jobroles/aboutCIW.asp?comm=CND&llm=2).

[5] Available at http://www.comptia.org/about/default.aspx.

[6] Available at http://www.learningtree.com/certification/index.htm.

[7] Available at http://www.novell.com/training/certinfo/.

[8] Available at http://education.oracle.com/pls/web_prod-plq-dad/db_pages.getpage?page_id=39.

[9] Available at https://www.redhat.com/training/rhce/courses/.

[10] Available at https://www.rsasecurity.com/node.asp?id=1261.

[11] Available at http://www.giac.org/.

[12] Available at http://www.sun.com/training/certification/java/index.xml.

[13] Available at http://www.symantec.com/enterprise/training/certification/symantec.html.

[14] Available at http://www.accessdata.com/training/ace/study_guide/.

[15] Available at http://www.certified-computer-examiner.com/.

[16] Available at http://www.leva.org/pages/CertificationAnnounce.htm.

[17] Available at http://www.guidancesoftware.com/training/ence/index.asp.

[18] Available at http://www.hightechcrimeinstitute.com/xcertification.htm.

[19] Available at http://www.iacis.info/iacisv2/pages/home.php.

[20] American Society of Crime Laboratory Directors/Laboratory Accreditation Board 2005 Manual. Published by ASCLD/LAB, June 2005, Gamer, North Carolina. pp. 61–68.

[21] Available at http://www.ascld-lab.org/legacy/aslablegacylaboratories.html.

Chapter 4

History, Concepts, and Technology of Networks and Their Security

Rebecca Gurley Bace

Summary

It is difficult, if not impossible, to imagine a world devoid of computers. We have, over the past half century, seen a culture evolve driven by the vision of "techno-magic", which allows us to perform everyday functions more easily, quickly, cheaply, reliably, and safely than we could when limited to manual means.

We remain, though, only human. As technology is staged in an environment still driven by human nature, the temptation to use its magical powers to less noble ends is irresistible. In an era when automobiles and aircraft are routinely involved in the conduct of criminal activity, it should come as no surprise that information networks and the computers that enable them are intrinsic to such activity as well. In this chapter, we will discuss the history and nature of computer and network technology, highlighting the fast-moving area of network security. As those charged with enforcing the law are themselves also dependent upon information technology, we will discuss the defensive as well as offensive aspects of this area.

Key Words: ARPA, Internet Protocol, OSI Model, Protocol stack, Rootkits, Spyware, TCP/IP, Trojan horse, firewall, intrusion detection, security policy.

1. A BRIEF HISTORY OF COMPUTERS AND NETWORKS

Computers have permeated most every aspect of our modern lives. Given this level of penetration, it is often a shock to realize that electronic computing devices are a relatively recent development. The original ENIAC projects of the 1940s marked the beginning of a steadily quickening march to our current state of automation, with the speed and memory capacity of computers growing by several orders of magnitude over this time.

From: *Handbook of Digital and Multimedia Forensic Evidence*
Edited by: J. J. Barbara © Humana Press Inc., Totowa, NJ

Early computer systems were huge programmable calculators, designed to perform complex calculations such as those associated with ballistics and other military concerns. These systems were centralized in design, with limited input, output, and storage options. Advances in the electronic components used to build computers, such as transistors and microprocessors, enabled significant improvements in the processing capacity of computer systems. At the same time, work in high-level programming languages and operating systems allowed increasing numbers of industries to utilize computers in their production operations. This created a thriving commercial market for computers and associated services. Still, for the first 30 years of computer technology, most computers were room-sized, requiring dedicated staffs to administer and operate them and significant accommodations (such as cooling systems and tightly controlled environments) to keep them operational. Furthermore, these systems were monolithic and could communicate with other systems by relatively primitive means. These mainframe systems comprised the first major generation of widely accepted computing devices.

2. Building the Internet

In the late 1960s, The U.S. Department of Defense's Advanced Projects Research Agency (ARPA) set forth on a research initiative to allow computers located at military installations to communicate with each other. One of the critical goals of this communications capability was extreme stability—this era was marked by the Cold War in which the presumed risk included nuclear weapons that could wipe out entire portions of the network. The stability was to come from the use of a new protocol (set of rules defining interactions between computers), then called the Network Communications Protocol (NCP). The initial computer network was called ARPAnet and linked four computer systems in four different locations.

ARPAnet expanded to include many thousands of systems over the life of the project. By the early 1980s, the Transmission Control Protocol/Internet Protocol (TCP/IP) protocol suite was published, representing a vast improvement over the original NCP. As the network grew, it began to take on some of the features of a society; for instance, specific communities of interest created their own "neighborhoods." Such subnets included Milnet, designed to serve the military, and NSFNet, designed to link five National Science Foundation–funded supercomputing centers and ultimately growing to connect all major universities. The ARPAnet was shut down in 1990, having been subsumed by the Internet as we know it today. The work performed in the ARPAnet project remains significant, as it yielded the components used to build the Internet. In Section 5.1, we'll take a closer look at TCP/IP, focusing on its design goals and structure.

3. A Reduction in Size: PCs, LANs, and the Microcomputer Revolution

If early computer mainframes and the ARPAnet defined computing in the large, two developments brought modern computing to the masses, bridging the "last mile." These two developments are the development of the personal computer (PC) and the development of the local area network (LAN) that links PCs to each other as well as to peripheral devices.

A number of microcomputers were brought to market in the early 1970s, but it was the IBM Personal Computer (PC), running the operating system Microsoft Disk Operating System (MS-DOS), that is credited with making computers available to individuals and small businesses. This served to launch a revolution. Given access to affordable computing platforms, software developers expanded the functional reach of computers, allowing large-scale use of computers for bookkeeping, word processing, education, recreation, and communications.

As the ARPAnet spawned a community of mainframe and large-scale computer users, the explosion in computing accessibility was amplified by the ability to link groups of computers together using LAN technologies. The earliest standard LAN was the Ethernet, created by a team at Xerox's Palo Alto Research Center during the early 1970s. The Ethernet protocol, which was cosponsored in its standardization by a consortium of firms including Xerox, Digital Equipment Corporation, and Intel, is now the de facto international standard for interconnection local networks.

4. UBIQUITOUS COMPUTING

Were we surveying the world of computing of the past few decades in "fast forward," we would spot several dominant trends developing over that time. First, computing devices have become cheaper, smaller, and less fragile. Second, computers have become far more communicative, in their interactions with humans and with other computers. Third, they have become far more powerful, with the speed and complexity of computer processors growing at exponential rates. Thanks to these and other advances, computers and computing networks have become truly ubiquitous in most of the civilized world. This ubiquity has transformed our lives in many ways, both good and bad, ensuring a steady supply of philosophical and social discussions for years to come. On a pragmatic note, many things in our modern lives, from cell phones to refrigerators, contain computers (complete with all the issues associated with computers). For the purposes of this discussion of information security, the ubiquity of modern computers is important because of the complexity of interactions across layers of computing devices and the complications in control that arise with such complexity.

5. NETWORK CONCEPTS

The world of data networking has worked hand in hand with developments in computing to create the online world in which we live. Computer networking has seen a relatively orderly path of progression, thanks in large part to the engineering rigor of those working on early network protocols. *Network protocols* are the standard rules defining how electronic devices communicate with each other.

5.1. TCP/IP

TCP/IP is the network protocol upon which the modern Internet is based. As the name might indicate, the TCP/IP protocol suite is composed of two separate protocols:

1. **TCP (Transmission Control Protocol).** The rules that govern how information is actually conveyed correctly over a data network (it includes provisions for error detection and correction by retransmission).

2. **IP (Internet Protocol).** The rules that govern how addressing is done across large internetworks (i.e., networks of networks).

There are numerous other protocols. Some common ones include Simple Mail Transfer Protocol (SMTP), which covers electronic mail; Simple Network Management Protocol (SNMP), which provides for common network management; and Domain Name Service (DNS), which defines how nodes on the Internet can be named. The Internet protocol is constructed using a layered model in which protocols are grouped into layers of abstraction, starting at the electrical hardware layer and proceeding upward to the point at which the user interacts with the system (application). A central concept of the Internet protocol is *encapsulation*, which means that protocols at higher layers of the model depend on protocols at lower layers of the model in order to perform their core functions. Thus, lower-layer protocols serve as building blocks for upper-layer protocols. This approach allows a networking protocol suite to knit together a wide variety of systems and networks such as required in the Internet. TCP/IP is divided into four layers:

1. **Link.** Handles passing of packets on two different hosts, and includes the physical hardware (hubs, repeaters, cables, connectors, network interface cards, etc.).
2. **Network.** Handles passing of packets across a single network. This layer also handles getting data from the source network to the destination network.
3. **Transport.** Handles passing of data from the Application to the Network layer. Transport layer protocols can be *connection-oriented* (e.g., TCP) in which data is conveyed in a byte stream or *connectionless* (e.g., UDP) in which data is conveyed in packet-sized datagrams. Transport layer protocols knit together communications between applications by using *ports*.
4. **Application.** Handles passing of data from software applications to the Transport layer. In other words, software applications that are designed to intercommunicate use the Application layer protocols to communicate over the network.

Another common model used to describe network interactions is the OSI (Open Systems Interconnection) reference model. The OSI model is specified in seven layers, as follows:

1. Layer 1: Physical Layer
2. Layer 2: Data Link Layer
3. Layer 3: Network Layer
4. Layer 4: Transport Layer
5. Layer 5: Session Layer
6. Layer 6: Presentation Layer
7. Layer 7: Application Layer

As in the TCP/IP model, each layer handles interactions between those protocols resident in the layers to either side of them. Also, there is not a crisp division between layers 2 and 3 (Data Link Layer and Network Layer, respectively), so some specify an additional layer "layer 2.5" to describe those protocols (e.g., MPLS, Multiprotocol Label Switching, is often classified as a layer 2.5 protocol.)

5.2. Protocol Stack

A *protocol stack* is the actual software that implements a protocol suite. The TCP/IP stack is usually divided into three sections, one for media (communicating with the hardware and wiring actually conveying the electrical communications signals), one for transport (stabilizing and then efficiently moving data across the network), and one for applications (granting access to network communications between software applications or programs). TCP/IP protocol stacks are a part of all but the most obscure operating system distributions today.

5.3. Ports

Under TCP/IP, there are special numbered entities called *ports* that are used by TCP and User Datagram Protocol, another of the core protocols of the Internet suite (UDP) to set up data communications between incoming data streams and running network processes on the receiving computer. Port numbers range from 0 to 65535 and are assigned by the Internet Assigned Numbers Authority (IANA); a part of the governance structure controlling the Internet, currently operated by the Internet Corporation for Assigned Names and Numbers, the non-profit corporation set up for the express purpose of managing the Internet (ICANN). Some ports that are assigned to common network functions include port 25 (assigned to SMTP, enabling e-mail); port 37 (assigned to the network time protocol); port 53 (assigned to DNS, the domain name service); and port 23 (assigned to Telnet).

6. SECURITY AND THE MODERN NETWORK

Security issues are a fixture of modern life, both online and off-line. In a world marked by technological progress, one might consider security issues to be an inevitable trailing effect of any significant advance. Using automotive technology as an analogy, think of how much of the automotive technology is driven by safety and security concerns. Furthermore, think of how much of the legislative and judicial energies of the United States and other modern nations are spent on issues arising from the use of automotive technology. The analogy is instructive in another key area—as the effects of network security breaches often affect all of us as individuals, it is important to understand the nature and substance of security problems.

6.1. What Is a Secure System?

In order to understand when security has been violated, it is helpful to first understand what we mean by the term *secure*. There are different ways of defining and characterizing security as it applies to digital systems. Let us take a look at both pragmatic and more theoretical definitions of system security.

One pragmatic definition of a secure system is "a system that can be trusted to behave as expected." This definition introduces another concept critical to the discussion of system security, that of *trust* , the confidence that the behavior observed corresponds with the behavior expected. Much of the practice of security centers on this notion of trust and how it is established, quantified, conserved, or destroyed over time.

A more classic, academic definition of security comes from the early work surrounding information security conducted under the auspices of the U.S. Department of Defense. This definition of security defines a secure system as one that possesses three properties, known as the "security triad," of Confidentiality, Integrity, and Availability:

1. **Confidentiality.** The requirement that access to information be restricted to only those users authorized for that access.

2. **Integrity.** The requirement that information be protected from alteration.
3. **Availability.** The requirement that information and system resources continue to work such that authorized users are able to access those systems and information when they need to, where they need to, and in the form they need to.

Others have expanded this list of relevant concepts to include notions of utility, authenticity, and access control, but for our discussion, the classic three are sufficient.

Another oft-ignored truth of security is that one needs to define what one expects from a system as part of defining security for that system. This introduces the concept of a *security policy*. A security policy is actually a balancing act, for a system's security policy includes both a management policy and a technical policy. The management policy is the statement articulating the desired security stance of a system. This policy is published as a set of management goals for security as well as a statement of the resources and processes management commits to achieving those goals. The technical policy is the actual set of security properties enforced by a system's security features. Comparing the desired security policy (as defined in the management policy) with the currently implemented technical security policy (as discovered and measured by vulnerability assessment processes) and closing the gap between them represents the core of security management.

6.2. Why Do Information Security Problems Occur?

Security problems exist in information systems for many reasons. Users who are frustrated by the number of security breaches that target their information often wonder why security professionals don't just fix the problem. One reason that they do not is that the problem does not lend itself well to quick fixes! To further understand the complexity of the problem, let us explore the causes of information security vulnerabilities. There are, in general, two precursors to security problems: vulnerabilities and threats. Among the most common causes of security vulnerabilities are the following:

1. **Problems in system design and development.**Systems must be designed to enforce security goals. If they are not, many coding errors and flaws will provide channels that an attacker can exploit to bypass any controls that exist.
2. **Problems in system management.** If systems are not managed in a security-smart fashion, they will not be secure. There are many examples of issues arising in this category, ranging from system administrators failing to enable security features (or worse yet, disabling those that are enabled by default), failure to establish appropriate security policy or failure to enforce existing policy, delaying security patching activity—all of these create vulnerabilities that can be exploited by adversaries.
3. **Problems in appropriately allocating trust.** If we are not realistic in assessing the trustworthiness of systems, there will be security problems. This can range from the purely business process (e.g., failure to do background checks on security-critical system administrators and users) to the purely technical (assumption that certain network protocols and services are secure, when numerous security issues and exploits are known/published).

Vulnerabilities are necessary; but not sufficient to in and of themselves represent security problems. Such problems occur when vulnerabilities are exploited via threats. A *Threat* is any situation or event that has the potential to harm a system. Threats include unauthorized parties who gain access to a system, authorized parties who exceed their legitimate access to files and resources on systems, and those who launch automated agents (i.e. software programs such as "worms" or "trojan horses") who act in either of the above fashions.

6.3. Should You Be Worried About Your Systems and Data?

It is a rare day when the morning newspaper does not allude to yet another major data breach involving the release of consumer credit card information and other sensitive information items from a commercial information system. Unless you are one of the many who are affected by identity theft or a targeted attack, it is tempting to assume that it does not matter whether or not your own systems are secured. The alternative would be to react violently to all online breaches, to gradually withdraw from all online activity, and to become a sort of recluse from the Internet.

But should you worry? Absolutely. Over the past decade, the level of criminal activity on the Internet has increased with incredible speed. Numerous instances are reported of organized criminals taking control of systems (and the personal information stored on those systems) and running extortion operations in which distributed denial of service (data flood) attacks are used to shut out legitimate customers before a key event. Many of these attackers install software "zombies" on home-based systems and use them in concert to run targeted attacks against victim sites. Reports abound of the attackers selling such zombie installations to others; maintaining zombie installations much as a farmer would raise livestock.

Perhaps more alarming, increasing numbers of exploits are reported in which people use online venues as platforms for nonelectronic crimes such as stalking or child victimization. Criminals take advantage of the lack of strong authentication and identity management systems by running "phishing" attacks. In these attacks, they send forged customer service e-mails from financial institutions that attract customers to a counterfeit online account access site. Once the customer attempts to log into the counterfeit site, his or her login information is captured or online activities subverted to the gain of the attacker.

Although a steady stream of new laws and regulations attempts to encourage financial institutions and other organizations with online presences to strengthen their security measures, these are slow remedies, subject to budget and manpower limitations. Promises to improve the security quality of software systems are made by the major vendors in operating system and application software. As security development tools and practices are still immature, these will result in slow, subtle improvements over time. Users must be more proactive in order to start protecting their systems now.

There are established practices that allow you to define your security goals for your systems, measure your exposure to various threats, and retain control over your networked systems. Especially if you are involved in professions or roles that involve access to sensitive data, be it intellectual property, court documents, financial information, or other sorts of controlled data, you cannot afford not to pay attention to securing this information when it is within your control.

There are many resources available to you that allow you to perform self-assessments of security exposures. There are Web-based vulnerability assessment services, as well as numerous open source and commercial security solutions available for most operating system environments. Many operating systems come complete with security features that allow you to limit the ability of others to install software on your system.

6.4. Where Do the Threats to Security Reside?

In assessing your exposure to network attack, it is helpful to characterize the security threats that are relevant to you. For instance, if you are running Red Hat Linux instead of Microsoft Windows, your security exposure will be significantly different. If you are running certain software applications, such as database management software, you may have security exposures associated with that specific software. If you travel extensively and rely on others for your network connectivity (e.g., WiFi network connectivity at the hotel coffee shop), your threat exposure will differ from the threat exposure in a classified government compound.

A critical differentiator for exposures is the sort of network connection your computer has to the Internet. If you rely on dialing into your network connection (i.e., the connection to the Internet is sporadic or "on demand"), your exposure to threats is quite different from that of someone whose system is connected to the Internet via a continuous high-speed link, such as DSL or cable service. In particular, if your system is connected continuously to the network, it may be subverted and used as an attack launching pad ("zombie").

6.5. What Sorts of Security Problems Are Issues?

There are many classes of security-related problems that may target your systems. A sampling of them includes:

1. **Viruses, worms, and other malicious code ("malware").** Viruses and worms are programs that are designed to perform various obnoxious operations on a victim system. They are different from other forms of malicious software (e.g., "Trojan horses") because they are designed to automatically reproduce themselves, spreading to other systems using networks and other channels for infection. In the case of viruses, some cooperation of a user is needed—running an application to which a virus is attached or opening a virus-infected e-mail message. In the case of worms, the process of identifying vulnerable hosts and infecting that host without direct user participation is usually integral to the worm's design (i.e., the worm scans the network for hosts with specific vulnerabilities, penetrates those systems by exploiting the vulnerability, then copies itself into the victim systems, launching itself to further spread).

2. **Trojan horses.** As in Homer's story of the gift from the Trojans that turned out to be an attack vector, a Trojan horse is a software program that provides "something extra" to you, in addition to or instead of those capabilities you intended. The most common Trojan horses are designed to give attackers a "back door" into your system, affect the system configuration (often disabling security measures), or destroy or alter specific data.

3. **Denial of Service (DoS) attack.** A DoS program is intended to affect the availability of your system and data. DoS attacks either render your system unstable (e.g., they crash your system) or else monopolize your data and system resources so that the system grinds to a halt. Network Denial of Service attacks, in which a "data storm" keeps legitimate users from accessing a network resource, have reportedly been used in extortion attempts against various online businesses.

4. **Mobile Code exploits.** Mobile code is code written by Web site developers designed to be executed by a Web browser accessing the site. Examples of programming languages used in mobile code development include Java, Javascript, and ActiveX. As mobile code is capable of allowing an adversary to perform unauthorized activities on a victim system ranging from surveillance of Web site accesses to launching malicious code, this class of problems is of great concern as Web use grows.

5. **Packet sniffing and other surveillance.** Most Ethernet Local area networks run in "promiscuous" mode—this means that unless networks are explicitly encrypted, all information traveling over the LAN is visible to anyone inclined to monitor the network. "Packet sniffers" capture information traveling over such network segments. This is of particular concern in cable network environments, as entire neighborhoods are often managed as single local area networks; thus, if you're accessing the Internet via a cable network connection, your network traffic may be visible to others using the same cable segment for access. This is of special concern as it may allow an adversary to capture userid-password pairs used to control access to corporate or commercial accounts.

6. **Spyware, rootkits, and other surveillance tools.** There are classes of software tools that exist for the purpose of allowing outsiders to take control of a system without the consent of the owner of that system. Spyware, though it originated as a surveillance mechanism, is ultimately a subversion attack in that it subverts the operation of a system to the benefit of a commercial interest or other third party. Rootkits, while enjoying some of the features and capabilities of spyware, add the capability of hiding themselves from discovery, thus allowing the controller of the rootkit to access and control the system undetected.

7. **Social engineering using technology vectors.** Some of the oldest scams in existence are seeing a revival in the online world. The financial world currently suffers from "phishing" attacks, in which criminals lure unsuspecting financial institution customers to forged Web sites in order to steal login and passwords (or other access credentials) from them—the criminals subsequently use the credentials to log into the user accounts and clean them out. There are similar instances of e-mails that attempt to enlist the "assistance" of innocents to help a displaced person regain some misplaced financial resources—the scam is a replay of a time-worn scam (known as the "Spanish Prisoner" in its original form, dating from the 1920s).

The above list is not comprehensive—the number and severity of specific threats have grown steadily over time with no end in sight. There are many excellent online sources of information security threats and resources. In particular, the federally funded CERT coordination center at Carnegie Mellon University (www.cert.org) offers a wide array of publications and advisories, from technical research papers to "how-to" manuals for nontechnical users. There is also a list of references at the close of this chapter that can provide additional information to the interested reader.

6.6. Tackling Security for Your Network

Lest we become depressed by the discussion of security threats, there is an important point to be made about the nature of security; it is not critical to understand each and every way your systems can be attacked. As mentioned previously, the cause of the vulnerabilities (often issues associated with the design and implementation process used to build the software applications on which we depend) is not necessarily under the control of users.

What *is* important is to understand the security fundamentals and management processes that will enable you to protect your system. This is analogous to being "street smart" as a part of controlling threats to your physical being. Thus, in the next section, we will shift our focus to the functional approaches to information security.

7. SECURITY PROCESSES

When people think about information security problems, they often wish for simple, one-shot cures. Many look for such remedies in the form of security products. Unfortunately, although good security products represent an important part of information system protection, they are not sufficient. Success in protecting systems depends on a sound, well-fitted process that defines how security products are to be used to protect a specific set of information systems.

The focus on process is based on a fundamental truth of modern life: without repeatable process, technology does not, indeed it cannot, scale to a larger world. The affordability of technology and all the benefits therein depend on scaling the costs of innovation across large populations of users (the drop in price for telephone service, Internet connectivity, even computers themselves attest to the success of this scalability). As in physical protection, the key to success in designing and implementing information security processes is to understand what assets exist within an environment, what value those assets represent, the nature of the threat exposures each of the assets faces, and what level of protection is appropriate for each. Once the needs are documented and budgets established, one can proceed to devising security architectures, policies and procedures, assign responsibility associated with protection of assets, and implement a security initiative within the organization in question, be it a household or a multinational corporation.

Let us step through such a security process, outlining the specific steps involved in devising a security plan and process. One might ask about where security policy fits within this picture. The security policy is the documentation of the philosophy of the organization regarding information security. It has associated practices and procedures that specify steps and resources that will be brought to bear in service of that philosophical set of security goals. Thus, the security policy is the "why" of security, and the process is the engineering road map for the implementation; that is, the "what" and "how."

7.1. Assessing Your Security Needs

The first step in any security process is to assess your general needs. To start, what system assets do you have? Make an inventory of systems, type of functions performed on each system (e.g., executive planning, finance, human resources), the criticality of information and function served by each system (i.e., what would happen if this system crashed and the information on it became unavailable?), and the level and nature of connectivity of each system.

Next, what information assets do you have? Make an inventory of information contained on each system, outlining specific types of information, the ownership of the information, the controls required for each type of information (legal, regulatory, and contract), the specific security exposures associated with each type of information, and the impact of security breaches involving the information.

Once this has been accomplished, look at the operational environments in which the information systems function. Are the systems (and the information on them) portable? What type of network connectivity applies to each system? How well managed are these network channels? Are operational environments attended round the clock? Are they monitored? Are appropriate physical security measures in place? Are there offsite backups for critical systems? Are appropriate operational standards (e.g., ITIL) in place? Are periodic backups of information stores standard practice? If so, how often are they done and how are the backups protected?

Finally, look at the human environment in which the information systems are operated. Who has ownership of (or ultimate responsibility for) each of the systems? Who has access to the systems? How are they authenticated (i.e., how do they identify themselves to the systems and how do the systems make sure that they are whom they say they are)? Are background checks done for personnel who have access to critical systems and information? Are there employment processes to curtail access to critical systems when employees are fired or otherwise denied system access for cause? What monitoring measures are present and who reviews logs and other monitoring information?

After gathering the background information, then one can proceed to the security-specific needs assessment. First, what are the security-related concerns that apply to the information and systems in this organization? Are they driven by:

1. **Regulatory and legal requirements?** Concerns that often arise are regulations such as the Sarbanes-Oxley Act (in the case of public corporations), The Health Insurance Portability and Accountability Act (HIPAA) in the case of health care information, Gramm Leach Bliley Act (GLBA) (in the case of financial organizations), and SB1386 (in the case of organizations doing business in California). All of these regulations mandate specific security and privacy-related practices for covered organizations. In the case of legal constraints, concerns regarding appropriate handling of digital evidence are often cited.

2. **Market environment and client concerns?** In certain commercial markets, (e.g., online financial institutions, e-commerce sites), security breaches result in loss of business as consumers become concerned about identity theft and other abuses involving their private information. In industries that compete for high-net-worth clientele, assurances regarding appropriate management of client information are essential to winning and retaining new business.

3. **Hostile operational environments?** As in the physical world, certain areas of the network are regarded as "bad neighborhoods" in which abuses are more numerous. Some of these neighborhoods are considered bad because of lax security practices (e.g., ISPs [Internet Service Providers] who tolerate spammers and others who abuse network access) and others are labeled as suspect because of organized criminal activity originating there.

Next, what threats apply to the systems and information within my scope of responsibility? Are there some that are unique to a particular operating environment? Working from the classic security threat models, for each type of information, determine:

1. **If confidentiality breaches are a problem.** Can this information be divulged to anyone besides a specific few?

2. **If integrity breaches are a problem.** What happens in this information is changed by an unauthorized party?

3. **If availability is a concern.** What happens if access to this information (or the system on which it resides) is denied?

Additionally, if the corporate concerns include market and client issues, you might add the following determinations:

1. **Is publicity surrounding an alleged security breach in and of itself an issue?**
2. **Is the organization subject to reporting requirements regarding security breaches?**
   Are there classes of protected information subject to law enforcement notification should they be breached?

At this juncture, you are at a point where you have a rudimentary understanding of the scope of your security process. It is now time to establish what you have to work with in tackling the needs you have articulated.

7.2. How Do I Satisfy My Security Needs?

In the inventories of systems, information, and responsibilities outlined in the sections above, hopefully you have established whether anyone has responsibility for security. If not, it is time to articulate the assets you need to appropriately protect your systems. Depending on the size of your organization and your access to security expertise and solutions, the resources and time required can range from hours to years. If you are in a small business, there are many ways to curb risk associated with information security without breaking the bank.

7.3. Commonsense Approaches to System Security

This section outlines steps that everyone can take to curb the risk of information security breaches, regardless of budget, expertise, or maturity of process. They represent elements of recognized best practices in information security.

1. **Perform system backups on a regular schedule**. Backups are a recognized cornerstone of good system management practice. Because so many security attacks seek to corrupt data within systems, frequent backups provide a way to survive such attacks while minimizing the pain of data recovery. There are numerous utilities that automate the backup process for various classes of machines. These, in combination with data protection mechanisms for locking down backup media, offer a great deal of security value with virtually no downside.
2. **Keep track of security patches for your operating system(s) and application software then download and install them as they become available**. Software vendors are usually quite responsive to reports of new vulnerabilities and issue software patches to close the vulnerabilities in reasonable time. Many of the most destructive broadscale security attacks target old vulnerabilities for which patches have been available for a long time. Managing patches across a large enterprise can be painful, but many commercial solutions exist (at a price) to ease that pain of deployment.
3. **Acquire and run a virus/malware detector.** The cost-benefit argument for security technology is perhaps strongest for this category of security application. The vendors for these tools take on the considerable work of searching for new virus forms, crafting signatures to search for them, and devising ways of blocking them at points of entry. Virus detectors are the information system equivalent of childhood vaccinations—the pain prevented by them is inestimable. Acquire them and use them.

4. **Manage identity intelligently**. In the case of systems in which you can opt for strong authentication (e.g., an authentication token or smart card vs. a userid-password), take the stronger authentication means. In situations where you deal with systems where strong authentication mechanisms are not possible, select userids and passwords that are stronger (i.e., harder to guess, include numbers and symbols, not published or written down in accessible locations) or use tools that assist you in managing those credentials.

5. **Be appropriately suspicious of unsolicited contact from the network world.** Do not open e-mail attachments unless you know the sender and, furthermore, are expecting them to send you documents. Do not click on Web site addresses and links in e-mail unless you know the sender and expect them to send you the reference in question. Do not *ever* give out your identification and authentication credentials (userid and password or equivalents) to anyone, especially via e-mail or telephone.

6. **Use the existing mechanisms for e-mail authentication (e.g., certificates and other credentials) when communicating with clients and commercial partners.** Consider using encryption mechanisms (including Virtual Private Networks) to secure messages and connections to corporate or other critical information systems.

7. **Use audit logging mechanisms and other audit mechanisms to log accesses to critical systems and information**. It is important to tune these mechanisms—assistance may be a good investment—but also important that once tuned, you set up a schedule to review the audit logs they produce, especially if you have a suspicion that your systems may have been breached. Note that if you are relying on systems for forensic analyses of evidence (that are subject to legal challenge), these audit logs can and should be augmented and tuned to document appropriate control over the analysis and storage platforms.

8. **Wireless networks represent an open door to the information systems of many businesses**. Unfortunately, given the broad, uncontested access such wireless networks offer, an open door can represent a huge security exposure. At a minimum, use WiFi Protected Access (WPA) mechanisms, not the security-flawed Wired Equivalence Privacy (WEP) mechanisms they replace, to restrict access to your system and wireless networks. These require that WPA be enabled at the wireless access point and that a passphrase be used to access the wireless network. The ability to control who accesses your wireless network is critical. Furthermore, when you use wireless networks in public settings (e.g., coffee shops and airports), be certain that you have protections in place to keep others on the same network from accessing your system (e.g., disable sharing of files across the network, use a personal firewall package to limit the entry or exit of information to/from your system, and do not access e-mail or other critical information unless you use an encrypted channel (e.g., SSL).

In summation, start with the most conservative security settings for your systems and networks, loosening them only when operational needs trump the needs for protection. And be conservative in determining when that trump card should be played.

8. LEGAL AND REGULATORY REQUIREMENTS FOR SECURITY

As mentioned previously, there are numerous legal and regulatory requirements that affect the design and implementation of information security. These can range from the abstract to the specific and tend to vary wildly depending on the location of the systems in question. Given the number and specificity of the regulations and laws in question, it is advisable to research the regulations applicable to your specific situation.

Pragmatic, actionable information regarding legal and regulatory compliance issues, practices, and resources are available through numerous Web sites that are designed for computer security officers and other information security professionals. In particular, the Web sites of *CSO Magazine* (www.csoonline.com) and Tech Target, publisher of *Information Security* magazine (www.searchsecurity.techtarget.com), are quite helpful in navigating the labyrinth of regulatory requirements.

When regulatory compliance is applicable to your specific situation, it provides a convenient measure of the budget you require for securing your systems. As regulatory agencies often levy significant fines for noncompliance, the requirement to bring systems into compliance has real quantifiable benefit to the organization. There is also a notion of industry-specific best practice (somewhat equivalent to the medical community's notion of "established standard of care") to define whether a certain set of security practices demonstrates sufficient diligence in protecting information assets. As regulations are often harmonized with current best practices, one could argue that by bringing systems into compliance with best practice, the benefit includes not only relief from fines and other such punitive measures but also some defense against negligence charges and associated litigation.

9. HANDLING SECURITY INCIDENTS

A final element in pulling together a security process and/or policy is that of defining the steps that should be carried out when a security breach occurs. This should document, as a minimum, the following items:

1. **Who has responsibility for what when a security incident occurs? In particular, who is the "go to" person users should contact when an attack is suspected?**
2. **What is involved in monitoring for breaches and how will you recognize that an attack is under way or has occurred?**
3. **Analysis and immediate response to the breach (including diagnosis, containment, eradication, restoring interim service, preservation of evidence).**
4. **Document the progress of the incident and your response to it.**
5. **Reporting the incident to users and other affected parties, including prescriptive measures to prevent recurrence of the incident.**

In addition to the pragmatic information listed above, incident handling planning affords you the luxury to explore certain issues associated with a serious or protracted attack. For instance, you can articulate:

1. **The escalation process for an extended or complicated attack.**
2. **The point at which law enforcement should be contacted.**
3. **The point at which employees, business partners, and customers are notified of an incident and how this notification will occur.**
4. **How, when, and by whom the media will be handled should news of the incident gain their attention.**

10. CONVERTING THE PROCESS TO ACTION

Though defining a security process is necessary, it is not in itself sufficient. The security process becomes real when you take the final steps to implement it. These steps are

1. **Identify responsible parties for each part of the process and take the necessary steps to enlist them.**
2. **Identify technology needs to appropriately protect your information assets and identify the assets necessary to acquire and integrate the technologies.**
3. **Go through whatever measures are necessary to acquire the assets necessary to implement the security process.**
4. **Devise a project plan for implementing the security process, gather your implementation team, and start marching.**

Understand that security is a living process—it evolves over time, taking on additional richness and relevance as it is applied and amended to reflect current information assets and threat environments. Thus, although you may reach local points of completion, it is important to reassess the needs of your organization on an ongoing basis.

11. FUTURE VIEWS

Some security experts assert that the old French saying *Plus ca change, plus ca la meme chose* (the common translation is "The more things change, the more they stay the same") best represents the nature of information security. Personally, after decades as a security researcher and practitioner, I prefer another quote: Roseanna Roseannadanna's: "It's always something." In a world in which technological advances arrive in a steady stream, the second-order effects of security issues inevitably follow. It is no more realistic to expect to "cure" security problems in one fell swoop than to expect to wipe out all auto-related injuries. What is realistic is to assume that new problems will surface. It is also realistic to expect that processes for assessing the real impact of security problems and mitigations will also evolve, driving corrective measures.

11.1. Looking Ahead

At times, it is hard to remember that computer and network technology, as well as the practice of information security, are still fledglings. There are numerous growing pains ahead of us, all representing great opportunity and great threat as well. Some of the trends are simply continuations of those already in progress.

First, it is clear that wireless networking and wireless communications in general will dominate our communications (and networking) infrastructure. This drives change in everything from network management to business models. The liberation from hardwired communications channels also changes the nature of computing and networking—one will be more dependent upon the information provided by the network even as one is subjected to problems associated with the reliability and integrity of that information and its source.

Second, many business services will be delivered "from the cloud." This marks a move away from maintaining an in-house IT operation, in favor of purchasing computing and network resources from a third party, much as we purchase telephone service from the telecommunications carriers today. This means that many corporate information assets will not be physically contained in onsite systems and that security and integrity of those offsite repositories will be even more critical than they are now.

Third, governments will continue to struggle with the time/distance warp associated with network connectivity and the move of financial resources to the Internet. Different governments will likely deal with the pressures in different ways, ranging from controls on encryption and data security measures to ubiquitous monitoring of all online communications. As in the physical world, some nations will establish themselves as safe havens for certain activities that are controlled in other political jurisdictions.

11.2. Changes in Threat Exposures

Threats will change as attackers become more technologically proficient. We will see a continuation of the current trends in which criminal elements increasingly use technical measures to accomplish traditional criminal goals—robberies, extortions, and fraud, to name but a few. The relative anonymity afforded by the online world will continue to serve as covering fire for illicit activities, and financial losses associated with cybercrime will grow steadily.

On the individual front, automated attacks will become more sophisticated and transparent, extending their reach into personal communications devices (e.g., cellphone/PDAs) and control Supervisory Control And Data Acquisition (SCADA) devices for industrial and commercial building control applications (e.g. heating, air conditioning, and plumbing controls). Public irritation regarding online crime will drive additional legal and regulatory requirements for security processes and technologies.

11.3. Changes in Security Measures

There will be advances on the security side as well. We will at last, driven by financial losses from identity fraud, see general acceptance of strong identification and authentication measures such as biometric and token-based schemes. We will also see a broadscale adoption of encrypted data storage devices and corporate data stores will likely be encrypted. Tamper resistance will be a standard fixture in certain classes of computerized control systems and may also serve as protection for certain security applications, adding a needed measure of assurance to them.

Virtual machine–based operating system architectures will become even more common and may serve as a powerful way of dealing with malware and other automated attacks. It is also possible that virtual machines (or substrate utility layers of software residing beneath them) will afford us the ability to monitor the operations of virtual machines in a way that is less subvertable than current auditing schemes.

After a generation of focus on protecting the infrastructure, the security products industry will focus on protecting information assets, the data itself. This move will put more pressure on security management tools, which allow one to orchestrate all the different protection mechanisms in play across an enterprise, but will result in advances in protection strategies.

Finally, the move to offload some security tasks to the providers of connectivity will continue and probably even accelerate. The expertise and time required to manage security in even a small business is such that users have indicated they will happily outsource it. In order for this trend to become ubiquitous, however, the security industry will devote considerable time and energy to establishing a means of measuring the security exposures of systems as well as the effectiveness of security management against those exposures.

Chapter 5

The Digital Crime Scene

Mark M. Pollitt

Summary

Digital Evidence: Information of probative value stored or transmitted in binary form *(1)*.

Modern society relies on electronic devices more and more. The Internet, computers, personal digital assistants (PDAs), cellular phones, and a wide variety of digital storage devices are part of most people's daily activities. It is no different for criminals. Therefore, we must anticipate the existence of digital evidence and be prepared to collect it from traditional sources as well as from new sources as they are developed and deployed.

Key Words: "Bag and tag," Digital crime scene, ECPA, Operations order, Search and seizure, SWGDE.

1. DIGITAL STORAGE DEVICES

In some ways, crime scenes involving digital evidence are no different than traditional ones. Their investigation requires planning, preparation, a methodical approach, and a set of specific skills. There are several areas where there are differences, such as the fact that the electronic evidence is physically located beyond the bounds of the search site. We will explore both the similarities and the differences in this chapter. However, one of the characteristics of digital evidence is that it is easily altered, damaged, or destroyed *(2)*, and doing so will negatively impact the evidentiary value of the seized items (Fig. 1). Therefore, the use of a trained digital evidence crime scene investigator *(3)* has become increasingly common.

From: *Handbook of Digital and Multimedia Forensic Evidence*
Edited by: J. J. Barbara © Humana Press Inc., Totowa, NJ

Fig. 1. Digital storage devices.

2. SEARCH PLANNING

There is an old adage about "prior planning prevents poor performance." It may well have been written about digital crime scenes. One search may be of a studio apartment with a single laptop computer whose relevance to the crime may be unknown. Another may involve a crime, such as hacking, facilitated by sophisticated computer users and involving a great deal of computer-related physical evidence, computers used to facilitate the crime, and perhaps many compromised remote computers. Yet a third might involve a significant fraud conducted by employees of a large firm where the evidence may reside on desktop computers, servers, and portable electronic devices. Each of these examples is manageable with proper planning.

2.1. Intelligence Collection

The earlier the digital crime scene investigator becomes involved in the case, the better. Digital evidence may be stored in a wide variety of forms, on different types of devices, and in different formats. The number and size of the devices will have a great impact on the time and number of people required to complete a search. Often, the scale of the search, the type of evidence, the volume of the evidence, the danger of that evidence being destroyed by a few keystrokes, and the technical complexity of the search may significantly shape the search execution.

In the law enforcement environment, a search begins with the legal authority to conduct the search. Is this search going to be done under consent, a regulatory authority, or under a search warrant? In each case, there will be requirements not only for predicating the search but also for its conduct. Further, there needs to be an assessment of whether there are any additional issues such as privilege, commingled data, or statutory protection of certain types of information. Search planners are responsible for the legality of the search as well as ensuring that all participants conduct themselves within the law.

In fact, experienced digital crime scene investigators can often assist the case investigator to develop a much more through and efficient search by providing options prior to the search. In some cases, the digital crime scene investigator may conduct some intelligence collection with the approval of the case investigator. This intelligence may be obtained from techniques such as pretext telephone calls or visits, online research, and interviews of informants, cooperating witnesses, vendors, and third parties. Although case investigators may have collected some of this information, often the digital crime scene investigator can add depth and context to that information.

It is useful to have a standardized list to guide the collection of presearch information. The following checklist is provided as an example. With experience, digital crime scene investigators develop customized lists of information critical to the types of searches that they conduct.

2.1.1. Example Intelligence Checklist

1. Summary of the case including the main and supporting suspects, violations being investigated, *modus operandi* (MO), and so forth.
2. How computers and electronic devices are being used in this case.
3. The technical sophistication of the subjects *(4)* and associates.
4. How the digital evidence is to be linked to specific subjects.
5. The type (office, home, data center, etc.), size, and layout of physical locations to be searched.
6. The potential for offsite storage of digital evidence in either physical or electronic storage (tape backups stored offsite) as well as their location (physical or network).
7. The type and size (both physical and in terms of storage) of electronic devices to be seized.
8. The operating systems, application software, and network environment.
9. The risk of destruction of some or all of the digital evidence.
10. Any potential legal issues involving the seizure of the digital evidence such as commingled data, privilege, or privacy protection.

2.2. Operations Order

The case and digital crime scene investigators should discuss the results of the intelligence collection and develop strategies for handling not only the probable scenario but also options should the environment change or not be found to be as anticipated. Issues such as the timing of the search (day or nighttime, knock, no-knock), manpower, and high- or low-profile conduct need to be carefully weighed. It is very important that the case and digital crime scene investigators have a shared understanding of the goals of the search, the priorities, and who will be responsible for decision making on scene. The goal of the planning phase is the development of an "Operations Order" that will be used to inform the participants of the process, assign responsibilities, and to manage the scene. Many law enforcement agencies have standardized forms for this purpose. If a standardized format does not exist, the digital crime scene investigator should consider developing one. Absent any standardized format, the use of a traditional military format such as the United States Marine Corps "Five Paragraph Order" *(5)* may be used.

At any crime scene, there are a number of things that need to be handled simultaneously. The physical scene must be protected, evidence must be searched for, subjects and witnesses need to be interviewed, and the entire process needs to be documented. The management of crime scenes is a much more sophisticated process than in years past. Specialization and division of labor have proved to yield much better results at crime scenes. Digital crime scene investigators are merely an additional area of specialization. With the inclusion of digital crime scene investigators, it is important to determine the specific responsibilities for each participant in the search and where they fit in the processing of the scene.

2.3. Search Preparation

Once the intelligence has been collected and the planning completed, it is important to collect the people and equipment needed for the search. Depending on the complexity of the planned search, the digital crime scene investigator may need additional personnel to assist in the process. Additionally, one of the most valuable resources that a digital crime scene investigator can bring to a scene is an address book with the contact information of as many technical specialists as possible. If the planned search has particular issues, it may be wise to seek out experts in that area who will make themselves available during the search. It is the crime scene investigator's responsibility to prepare the other technical participants for the planned operation.

The need for specialized equipment and tools is one of the aspects that set apart digital crime scenes from other searches. There are two fundamental approaches to executing a search for digital evidence: "bag and tag" and onsite seizure/imaging. The former refers to the seizure of physical objects, such as computers, disks, and other storage media. Usually, no attempt is made to conduct an onsite review or examination of the objects. However, in some limited circumstances, evidence may be previewed in order to eliminate unnecessary seizures. It must be stressed that if a preview is done on scene, it is done by qualified personnel using forensically sound tools that will preserve the integrity of the evidence.

In cases where a "bag and tag" will be conducted, the digital crime scene investigator needs to ensure that there are adequate supplies to secure the evidence (Table 1). Generally, paper bags or static-free plastic bags are best for the collection of magnetic

Table 1
Suggested list of equipment for "bag and tag" searches

Forms and notepaper	Cardboard boxes
Evidence tape	Indelible markers (fine point)
Evidence tags/labels	Flashlights
Manila envelopes (6 × 9, 9 × 12)	Static-free bubble wrap
Plastic bags (for cables, etc.)	Latex or rubber gloves
Static-free bags	Digital camera

media such as hard drives. The use of ordinary plastic bags should be avoided due to static discharge issues as well as moisture control. Optical disks, such as CD-ROMs and DVDs, will sometimes adhere to each other when there is trapped moisture in a plastic bag. Bags containing multiple pieces of evidence should be counted and recounted in order to ensure that a correct count is recorded on the container and on the evidence log. Some practitioners go so far as to photocopy or digitally photograph all of the objects before they are placed in a container. Direct marking with an indelible pen is a very effective method, but care must be taken to ensure that the media is not damaged or that the optical surface is not defaced. Both tamper-evident and removable evidence tape are commonly used in connection with digital evidence. The tamper-evident tape is used to secure bags and boxes, and the removable tape is used to bundle cables and wires. Various sizes of cardboard boxes, adhesive evidence labels, and string labels are also useful.

Searches, especially when the original equipment is not going to be seized but copies of files or forensic duplicates (images) are going to be created, must be very thoroughly planned. A clear understanding of the type of computers and digital storage devices, their interfaces, and the amount of data to be copied is crucial to success. Sufficient sterile (forensically wiped) media must be available before the search begins. In cases where on-scene imaging, that is, the forensic duplication of digital media, is to be done, it is necessary to have adequate imaging hardware, including spares and a range of interfaces to deal with a wide variety of hardware. It is often necessary to use alternate methods of duplication in order to copy a given piece of storage media. Digital crime scene investigators must plan for the unexpected. Also, where large numbers of computers or physically large amounts of storage media are to be seized, it is necessary to have adequate transportation for the seized objects.

2.4. The Search Briefing

Prior to conducting a search, good practice suggests that a briefing, preferably a formal one, be held to ensure that the search is conducted in an efficient, legal, and safe fashion. In addition to covering the operations order, time is usually made available for questions or issues. This provides the digital crime scene investigator an opportunity to enlist the assistance of the other search team members and to educate them concerning digital evidence–related issues.

The other search participants can be encouraged to look for digital storage devices, logs, notebooks, and pieces of paper that may contain user names, account numbers, and/or passwords. Interviewers can be encouraged to question subjects and witnesses concerning their computer use, accounts, usernames, and passwords. It may be that these interviews will provide the critical link between a given piece of digital evidence and the subject of the investigation. The digital crime scene investigator, by identifying themselves as such, can serve as a resource to the other search participants.

2.5. The Search Process

The search process can generally be defined as initial entry, sweep and survey, documentation, search, seizure, and departure. It is suggested that the Operations Order address each of these phases specifically with specific individuals assigned to tasks in each phase.

2.5.1. Entry

The authority and responsibility for the entry onto the premises is that of the case investigator. Depending on the type of case and location, the entry may be as simple as the investigator walking into a business during working hours and serving the warrant. At the other end of the spectrum is a tactical entry into a secured location by a SWAT team. Usually, the entry is conducted by sworn personnel and, except in rare situations, there is not a need for the digital crime scene investigator to participate in the entry.

2.5.2. Sweep and Survey

Generally, the physical protection of the crime scene and control of the occupants will be performed by sworn personnel. Usually, a "protective sweep" of the entire premises will be conducted to ascertain if there are any physical threats to the safety of the search party. Anyone present must immediately be moved away from all computers and other electronic devices. Consideration may be given to restricting access to cell phones and other portable electronic devices. Thereafter, they will secure the site to preserve the search scene.

The next part of this phase is to conduct a "walk through" to determine the actual situation in order to ensure that no evidence is at risk for alteration or destruction and to make necessary adjustments to the Operations Order. The digital crime scene investigator needs to either accompany the case investigator or conduct a survey separately. One of the duties of the digital crime scene investigator is to ensure that none of the digital evidence is at risk due to malicious software, physical access by subjects, or remote access. Computers and other electronic devices that are operating at the time of the sweep must be evaluated for the risk of data loss. During the sweep, the digital crime scene investigator may need to make a quick decision concerning whether to immediately shut down the computer system or to allow it to remain operating (see Section 2.5.4).

The digital crime scene investigator also uses this opportunity to develop a strategy and priority for the collection phase. Often, it will be useful to take notes of the digital evidence items in plain view during this sweep. It will allow the digital crime scene investigator an opportunity to provide input, such as things to search for, to the individuals who will be responsible for the search of that area. Based on this survey, the digital crime scene investigator may need to request that the case investigators conduct specific interviews *(6)* or that previously agreed upon priorities or assignments be adjusted.

2.5.3. Documentation

At the end of the initial survey, the initial documentation of the crime scene begins, often by doing a sketch of the crime scene and taking the "before" photographs. The digital crime scene investigator should work with the crime scene photographer to get a series of photographs of each computer area in progressively more detailed views. This may allow for investigators and/or the digital evidence forensic examiner to testify concerning how the computer may have been used. It also aids in the identification of the computer.

In searches of more than one room, letters or numbers will generally be assigned to rooms in accordance with the organization's standard practice (Fig. 2). Often, these

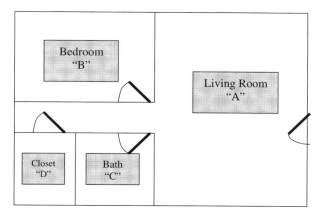

Fig. 2. Crime scene sketch.

letters or numbers are subsequently used in numbering the seized evidence. If the living room is designated "room A," then the first piece of evidence seized there will be A-1.

Normally, access is restricted to the search area until the sketches and photographs are completed. Once these are finished, the actual search begins. Whereas all search team members must be aware of potential evidentiary items (able to identify or perhaps seize items of digital evidence), it will often be the digital crime scene investigator who conducts the seizure of the computers. Regardless, care should be taken to carefully photograph, from wide-angle down to a photograph of a single item, and document the material in the vicinity of any computers. Experience has shown that the closer items are to the computer, the more likely they are to be information that is important and current. Another practice that may prove useful in the postsearch phase is to seize, mark, package, and enter all items that are related to a particular computer as separate evidence items. This will allow for the easy identification and retrieval of computer-related evidence without the need to check out more material than needed or "splitting" items in the evidence control system.

2.5.4. Operating Computer Systems

When investigators enter crime scenes, they often find computer systems that are up and running. They may observe activity taking place on the monitor's screen, lights illuminated indicating that power is applied, or lights indicating activity of either storage devices or a network. The digital crime scene investigator, in consultation with the case investigator, must make a decision how to proceed. First, consideration should be given to whether the device is relevant to the investigation, is it likely to contain probative information, and what are the consequences of shutting down the device. The decision must also take into consideration the environment: home office, hospital, and so forth.

If it is determined that shutting down the device(s) is necessary or prudent, a decision must be made as to how the shutdown will be implemented. Generally, there are two approaches: one referred to as "clean" in which the system is powered down in normal fashion and the other called "dirty" in which the power is abruptly removed.

The decision must balance the potential loss of evidence from deletion or alteration should immediate shutdown not be undertaken against the potential for the loss of unsaved data or data being corrupted from doing a "dirty" shutdown.

A complete discussion of all of the technical aspects of "dirty" versus "clean" shutdowns is beyond the scope of this chapter. The decision on whether or not to shut down a system and how to do so should be made in a rational fashion, weighing the options and documenting the reasons in the crime scene notes. It is this author's opinion that, absent objective evidence to believe any malicious activity is either happening or likely, a "clean" shutdown has the best chance for preserving the largest amount of evidence. It does need to be emphasized that this decision must be made on a case by case basis using the information known to the investigators.

Should the decision be made to conduct a "clean" shutdown, the following procedure is recommended:

1. Document the date and time of each step. Include the computer's system time if displayed.
2. Photograph or videotape the process. Back this up with detailed notes.
3. Photograph each page of any open document before attempting to close or save.
4. Consider saving all open documents to forensically sterile media. If removable storage devices are to be attached, record the date, time, make and model in order to document changes to system files.
5. Note the system time when files are saved and then closed.
6. Repeat for each open item.
7. Shut down the system using the normal shutdown procedure for the operating system and hardware.

2.5.5. Safety Issues

There are a number of safety issues with regard to digital evidence. For both safety and evidence preservation reasons, nothing electrical should be turned on unless it is by a qualified digital evidence specialist and only if necessary to complete the search. Items that are powered on at the time of the search may remain "on" (subject to evidence preservation issues) until it is time to seize the items.

Computer equipment is often made of sheet metal and plastic. Manufacturers usually do not round the edges and corners of the metal cases. Thus, great care should be exercised when handling any open computer cases. Virtually every experienced digital evidence specialist has received painful and sometimes serious injuries from razor-sharp sheet metal.

Consideration may be given to handling any keyboards for latent fingerprint, hair and fiber, or DNA evidence. Experience has shown that keyboards collect large quantities of this type of evidence, which can easily be collected and preserved by placing the keyboard in a paper bag. Even if keyboards are not being preserved for evidentiary purposes, experienced practitioners prefer to handle keyboards using gloves to prevent contact with biological contaminants.

2.5.6. Seizure

Once items of digital evidence have been identified, determined to be potentially relevant to the investigation, and subject to seizure under the operative legal authority, they may be seized. There are three objectives to this stage: positive identification of the seized item, establishment of the chain of custody, and protection of the evidence from deleterious change.

Items of digital evidence may take many forms, from individual disks to entire computer systems including printers and other externally connected devices. Items may be grouped together or identified individually. Consideration should be given to keeping like items together while allowing for the easy retrieval from evidence storage of all material related to a single computer system.

Thus, a number of optical disks (CD-ROMs or DVDs) located on a table might be photographed together, separated into those with commercial labels and those with hand-written notations, and placed into respective bags. A computer system consisting of a central processing unit (the "computer" case), keyboard, and monitor might be processed as a single item, that is, "A-1" (for room A, item 1) with the central processing unit marked "A-1-a," the keyboard "A-1-b," and the monitor "A-1-c."

Marking of digital evidence may be done directly on the item using an indelible marker, adhesive label, and so forth, or indirectly, that is the items are placed in a bag or container that is then marked (Fig. 3). Care must be taken when marking items directly to ensure that their functionality is not impaired. Experience has shown that tamper-evident tape can seriously compromise the electromechanical aspects of removable storage items such as floppy disks and connectors and should be avoided. Indelible markers should never be used to mark the storage surface(s) of optical disks,

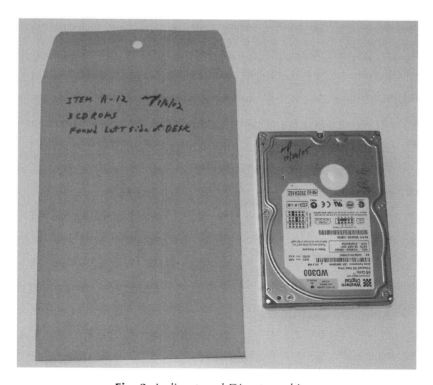

Fig. 3. Indirect and Direct marking.

and adhesive labels should generally not be applied to removable or optical disks in order to prevent fouling the drive mechanisms or creating an imbalanced disk.

It is often important to capture the physical configuration of the computer at the time of seizure. That is to say: was it connected and what other devices were attached? Computer systems should be photographed before marking, again after marking, again with the connectors marked; all before being disassembled. The labeled cables may then be placed in a bag, which will be marked as described above.

The labeling of the cables should allow for subsequent re-creation of the computer system as found. The accepted practice is to label each connector and the place where it was attached. This can be done using numbers, letters, or a combination of both. Whatever scheme is chosen, it must be consistent and allow for the connection of the correct end of the cable to the correct device (Fig. 4).

2.5.7. Departure

Usually, there is a legal requirement to provide the owner of the location being searched with an inventory of the items seized as well as a copy of the search warrant, if applicable. This is typically the responsibility of the case investigator. If the digital crime scene investigator seized (downloaded or copied) information from online systems, then that information must be included in the inventory.

A final sweep should be conducted to ensure that no potential evidence has been overlooked or left behind. Also, this will ensure that all notes, equipment, identification, cell phones, and so forth, belonging to the search party are not left behind either. After this sweep is conducted, the photographer should take a series of exit photos documenting the state of the search scene.

2.6. Searches in the Private Sector

The fundamental difference between digital evidence searches in a law enforcement context and those undertaken in the private sector is the underlying authority and the constraints that devolve from that authority. What does not change is the core methodology in conducting the search. The paperwork may read differently and the

Fig. 4. Marking computer connectors.

terminology may be slightly different, but the process remains essentially the same. In this section, we will look at both the authority and the process.

Searches in the private sector are common as a result of some civil law relationship; employment, contractor, or customer. These relationships can either explicitly or implicitly give parties rights in these relationships that can be enforced according to either the contract or under civil law. Under the terms of our employment, we are obligated to follow the policies issued by our employers. Our employment is a contract where we work and the employer pays us. Our failure to perform can result in our termination for just cause. Employers need to conduct sufficient investigation to develop documentation that will support the termination and to defend itself against a civil lawsuit challenging that employment decision. Likewise, suppliers and many other business partners are subject to the terms of sometimes very detailed contracts that may include the right to inspection of the contractor's corporate records. Customers have certain rights under both common law and statute that may allow them to sue vendors for civil wrongs called torts. Business entities have the right to defend themselves and their property under civil law as well. It is important to note that civil torts may also be crimes under the criminal law. It is not unusual for information collected for one of these purposes to be used in connection with the other type of legal proceeding.

It is important to establish, up front, the authority under which a given search is being conducted. Is this an internal search that is designed to protect the company's information systems from an outside hacker or is it a personnel investigation to determine if an employee is violating corporate policy? It may be well to contact corporate counsel to clearly establish the basis and any limitations upon the proposed search activity. It is also important to determine affirmatively that the proposed search conduct will not violate any criminal laws such as the Wiretap Statute *(7)* or the Electronic Communications Privacy Act (ECPA) *(8)* and does not create the potential for any unacceptable liability.

In terms of process in the corporate world, perhaps the best search is not a search at all but rather the collection of information that is done in the normal course of business and used for a business purpose. In legal terms these are called *business records* and are routinely admitted into court under the business records exception to the hearsay rule *(9)*.

This argues for the routine collection and preservation of security-related information that may become material to a civil or even criminal matter. Searches that are conducted in response to a specific situation need to be planned and executed just as carefully as those conducted in the criminal area. The clear delineation of authority, the careful planning, the consideration of operational issues, the methodical approach, and the meticulous execution and documentation are just as important in the private sector as in the public. In fact, it may even be greater, as searches for digital evidence may be far more infrequent in the private sector.

Additional Readings

NIJ Electronic Crime Scene Investigation: A Guide for First Responders. Available at http://www.ojp.usdoj.gov/nij/pubs-sum/187736.htm.

U.S. Department of Justice Guide to Searching and Seizing Computers and Obtaining Electronic Evidence in Criminal Investigations. Available at http://www.sbot.org/library/SearchingandSeizingComputers_7_02.htm.

Casey, E. *Digital Evidence and Computer Crime*, 2nd ed. New York: Academic Press, 2004.

REFERENCES AND NOTES

[1] Scientific Working Group on Digital Evidence SWGDE and SWGIT Combined Master Glossary of Terms. Available at http://www.swgde.org.

[2] National Institute of Justice Electronic Crime Scene Investigation: A Guide for First Responders. Available at http://www.ncjrs.gov/txtfiles1/nij/187736.txt.

[3] For the purposes of this chapter, the term *digital crime scene investigator* will be used to represent anyone, sworn or nonsworn, who is assigned specifically to conduct searches for digital evidence.

[4] The term *subjects* is used in this chapter to denote someone of investigative interest. These individuals may or may not be suspected of a crime.

[5] Paragraph Order (SMEAC):

> *Situation*: describe what the current situation is.
>
> *Mission*: describe what the current mission is.
>
> *Execution*: describe how the mission will be carried out.
>
> *Administration and Logistics*: describe how administrative duties and logistical support will be handled.
>
> *Command and Signals*: describe who the persons in authority are and any special signals that need to be recognized.

Available at http://www.leatherneck.com/forums/archive/index.php/t-324.html.

[6] Digital crime scene investigators may, with the agreement of the case investigator and subject to department regulations, conduct interviews. It is suggested that, should the digital crime scene investigator not be sworn, that the interview be conducted by sworn personnel with the digital crime scene investigator participating. Regardless of the digital crime scene investigator's status, it is recommended that this interview be separately documented from the search and any on-scene examination.

[7] 18 U.S.C. § 2510 et seq.

[8] 18 U.S.C. § 2703 et seq.

[9] See Federal Rule of Evidence 803(6).

Chapter 6

Investigating Cybercrime

Philippe Dubord

Summary

It is beyond the scope of this chapter to discuss in detail every cybercrime being committed. Rather, this chapter discusses two major categories of cybercrime committed with the use of technology: *online child exploitation* and *online fraudulent theft*. In recent times, we have seen the emergence of individuals and organized groups using technology to exploit children, for theft of personal information, stalking, fraud, terrorism, espionage, and a host of other types of crimes. The law enforcement community has made huge advances in combating cybercrime by providing investigators ongoing advance training in cyberinvestigation, formulation of federal, state, and local task forces, and cooperation with their international counterparts. Because the Internet is worldwide with local jurisdictions, it becomes necessary for law enforcement to pull together and share resources to identify, arrest, and prosecute the criminals using this technology.

Key Words: Child pornography, Computer intrusion, Cybercrime, Hacker, NCMEC, Phisher, US-CERT.

1. ONLINE CHILD EXPLOITATION: CHILD PORNOGRAPHY

Cybercrime (or high-tech crimes) are not unique in the sense that they are new types of crimes, but mainly they are traditional crimes committed with the use of computer technology. New laws have evolved from technology over the past years due to criminals finding ways around existing laws to conduct their illegal activity. Of great concern to law enforcement today (and also to the general public) is the proliferation of child pornography over the past several years. It can be stated that its prevalence is a direct result of all that latest technology directed toward an insidious purpose.

From: *Handbook of Digital and Multimedia Forensic Evidence*
Edited by: J. J. Barbara © Humana Press Inc., Totowa, NJ

1.1. Working Definition

Any investigators assigned to work a potential child pornography investigation need to have an understanding or a definition of what can be considered potential child pornography. This is especially true if the investigator is new or inexperienced in conducting this type of investigation. A practical, working definition that is all inclusive for child pornography can be summarized: "the depiction of minors engaged in sexual activity and/or posed in a lewd and lascivious manner exhibiting the child's genitalia." An essential component is the "posed in a lewd and lascivious manner exhibiting the child's genitalia." This definition would tend to exclude children who may be seen or photographed in a "naturalist environment" or those commonly seen running around nude on a beach.

1.2. Legal Definition

In contrast with the working definition is the much more defined, legal definition of child pornography. As stated in the U.S. Code, child pornography is defined as: "any visual depiction, including any photograph, film, video, picture, or computer or computer-generated image or picture, whether made or produced by electronic, mechanical, or other means, of sexually explicit conduct, where, (a) the production of such visual depiction involves the use of a minor engaging in sexually explicit conduct; (b) such visual depiction is, or appears to be, of a minor engaging in sexually explicit conduct; (c) such visual depiction has been created, adapted, or modified to appear that an identifiable minor is engaging in sexually explicit conduct; or (d) such visual depiction is advertised, promoted, presented, described, or distributed in such a manner that conveys the impression that the material is or contains a visual depiction of a minor engaging in sexually explicit conduct" (U.S.C. Title 18 section 2256).

Individual states define and classify child pornography differently. For example, in California it is a misdemeanor to possess child pornography. In contrast, under Florida statutes, it is a felony to possess child pornography. Furthermore, Florida law concerning child pornography is titled "Sexual Performance by a Child" which is defined as: "It is unlawful for any person to knowingly possess a photograph, motion picture, exhibition, show, representation, or other presentation which, in whole or in part, includes any sexual conduct by a child. The possession of each such photograph, motion picture, exhibition, show, representation, or other presentation is a separate offense. Whoever violates this subsection is guilty of a felony of the third degree" *(1)*.

In various other countries, child pornography laws do not exist. A study conducted by the International Centre for Missing and Exploited Children (ICMEC) found that "possession of child pornography is not a crime in 138 countries. In 122 countries, there are no laws dealing with the use of computers and the Internet as a means of child pornography distribution" *(2)*.

Penalties for child pornography vary from state to state. In the federal judicial system, individuals convicted of these types of crimes receive mandatory sentences. In most federal child pornography offenses, if a person is convicted of distributing child pornography, they will receive a minimum 5-year sentence, or up to 10 years in prison, depending upon other circumstances. Individuals charged with one count of producing child pornography can receive a minimum sentence of 15 years in prison.

1.3. Technology's Impact on Child Pornography

Generally speaking, technological progress and advancement is valued by society. However, it seems that every technological advance is quickly embraced by offenders for illegal purposes, particularly when applied to child pornography. For example:

1. Digital cameras are affordable and carry no risk to the owner of the fear of being discovered in external film development.
2. Everyone has access to vast amounts of child pornography via the Internet.
3. Photographs and movies are easily organized, concealed, and stored in a user's collections.
4. Use of chat rooms, e-mail, and so forth, allows offenders to reach out to like-minded individuals to validate their deviant behavior and activities.
5. Many children congregate on the Internet in social networks giving offenders a large potential victim pool.
6. Perceived anonymity.
7. No boundaries.

Prior to the development of the Internet and the technological advances cited above, offenders risked being caught by having to order illegal material from overseas via mail and/or arranging to meet a like-minded individual in person to trade and/or purchase illicit materials. Today, offenders, in the comfort of their homes and with only a couple clicks of the mouse, can access numerous areas of the Internet where child pornography is available.

In the mid-1990s when the Internet was growing by leaps and bounds, newsgroups, also known as UseNet and described as "electronic corkboards," were popular with offenders seeking child pornography. Individuals posted (uploaded) files to a specific newsgroup for others to see and/or download. Today, there are several types of newsgroups with topics for almost everyone, from posting erotic pictures depicting teens to recreational food cooking. Many Internet Service Providers (ISPs) filter newsgroups from their news servers that are suspected to contain offensive and/or illegal materials. Quite obviously, that has not stopped other Internet entrepreneurs from providing, for a fee, uncensored newsgroups. It is estimated that more than 100,000 newsgroups are currently available.

As the Internet continues to evolve, offenders have discovered a chat and file transfer program called Internet Relay Chat (IRC). This program is free and makes it possible for individuals to create fictitious screen names as well as to chat and transfer files. Offenders learned that they could set up an IRC client, for example, MIRC (www.mirc.com). Created by Khaled Mardam-Bay in 1995, it is currently one of the most popular IRC clients. It can easily be configured to automatically send and receive files (known as a file server and also known as an f-server). Typically to set up an f-server, the individual needs an Internet connection, the IRC client, and the f-serve script. For example, Panzer, which is an f-serve script, allows you to keep file ratios, download stats, upload stats, monitor incoming files and channel advertising systems.

This method became, and still is, very popular with child pornographic traders and collectors, primarily due to the automated delivery and receiving of child pornography and a near risk-free environment. In essence, the offender can launch the IRC client, engage the f-serve script and enter a chat channel (e.g., "preteensexpics"), advertising their f-server and then leave for work. Upon their return, their computer has received hundreds of child pornography image files from other individuals on the IRC network.

In the past several years, Peer-to-Peer (P2P) technology has taken file sharing to the next level. These file-sharing programs, such as Napster (www.napster.com), Kazaa (www.kazaa.com), and Limewire (www.limewire.com), became very popular with teens due to the ability to download large volumes of music files (MP3s) for free along with chatting capabilities. Napster was one of the first file-sharing programs that functioned on a central server. Current file-sharing programs like Limewire and Kazaa are built on a decentralized server model. The offenders once again found a new avenue to obtain and distribute child pornography through file-sharing networks. The file-sharing programs are easy to use and allow the offender to feel anonymous to the world.

Child pornography is not only being traded among individuals with a sexual interest in children, but it has become a multibillion dollar a year criminal enterprise. Law enforcement has investigated numerous commercial child pornography Web sites that lead to Russia and surrounding countries. Senator Richard Shelby, then chairman of the Senate Banking Committee, discovered that "some money paid for child porn ends in the hands of international crime groups like the Russian Mafia" *(3)*. These criminal groups know that newer child pornography is constantly being sought by individuals interested in this material and are producing child pornography for profit, which means children are continuing to be victimized.

2. ONLINE CHILD EXPLOITATION: SOLICITING CHILDREN FOR SEX

Another cybercrime that did not previously exist is that of soliciting children for sex. Technological progress has made this crime easier for the offender to commit. The offender can solicit sex via his or her computer or by using his or her new cellular telephone that allows direct connections to the Internet and/or chat rooms.

2.1. Working Definition

Similar to child pornography, the investigator needs to have an understanding of both a working definition of what can be considered solicitation and a legal definition for prosecution purposes. A simplified working definition can be stated as follows: the offender "knowingly lured, seduced and or enticed a child via the Internet to engage in sexual activity, or attempted to do so." It is important to note that under the working definition, "or attempted to do so" can be critical to an investigation or an arrest.

2.2. Legal Definition

Again, similar to child pornography, the legal definition is much more defined. From the U.S. Code: "Whoever, using the mail or any facility or means of interstate or foreign commerce, or within the special maritime and territorial jurisdiction of the United States knowingly persuades, induces, entices or coerces any individual who has not attained the age of 18 years, to engage in prostitution or any sexual activity for which any person can be charged with a criminal offense, or attempts to do so, shall be fined under this title, imprisoned not more than 15 years, or both" *(4)*.

The legal definition mentioned above covers federal violations. Individual states have enacted similar laws but have different titles and elements. For example, Florida law titles this offense as "Computer Pornography" and defines it as a person who

> knowingly complies, enters into, or transmits by use of computer; makes, prints, publishes, or reproduces by other computerized means; knowingly causes or allows to be entered into or transmitted by use of computer or buys, sells, receives, exchanges, or disseminates, any notice, statement, or advertisement of any minor's name, telephone number, place of residence, physical characteristics, or other descriptive or identifying information for the purposes of facilitating, encouraging, offering, or soliciting sexual conduct of or with any minor, or the visual depiction of such conduct, commits a felony of the third degree, punishable as in statutes 775.082, 775.083 or 775.084. The fact that an undercover operative or law enforcement officer was involved in the detection and investigation of an offense under this section shall not constitute a defense to prosecution under this section *(5)*.

2.3. Technology's Impact on Soliciting Children for Sex

Individuals who have the desire to meet children for sex have learned to navigate the Internet very well to seek out areas where children tend to congregate online. Again, the offender does not have to spend hours or days looking for potential victims at malls, parks, and other places children tend to hang out. In the comfort of the offender's home and with a couple clicks of a mouse, the offender has time and little or no fear of being caught victimizing children on the Internet.

Some of the common areas Internet predators seek out children are in social networking sites. For example, chat rooms are very popular with both children and, unfortunately, with predators. As Internet chatting was becoming one of the most popular means for the world to communicate, programs such as MIRC were utilized. Due to MIRC's multiple functions and no true monitoring of its content and users, it fast became the offender's tool of choice. The chat channels are created by the users and can be named practically anything. Usually, chat channels are named to describe the activity in that channel, for example, "dads and daughters."

Other Internet chat services soon emerged into the mainstream of cybercommunications. Yahoo Messenger, America Online Instant Messenger (AIM), "I Seek U" (ICQ), and MSN Messenger are some examples. Law enforcement soon discovered that predators were using multiple chat services to seduce and/or groom children. These newer chat services, which also integrated Web cameras and voice capabilities, made them more attractive to predators. The predators now can see and hear the children they are trying to lure into their perverted world. An analogy of a Web camera activity by some of these predators can be equated to the suspect in the trench coat standing on a corner exposing themselves to children at the bus stop.

As newer technology is released, children sometimes tend to get involved without considering the consequences of their actions. This is currently happening with the Web logs, also known as "blogs," which are personal Web sites containing regular updated entries displayed in reverse chronological order. They read like a diary or a journal, but with the most recent entry at the top. The most current and controversial blog site is Myspace.com (www.myspace.com). School-aged children, typically in the middle to higher grades, are placing personal information about themselves and others on these blog sites. The type of information routinely seen includes full disclosures of their name, location, phone numbers, school, activities, likes, dislikes, and so on. Along with personal information, children are posting numerous photographs of themselves and others, making these sites "one stop" shopping for predators. Predators can find one child's blog and view all the child's friends who have posted messages or are listed. If one child doesn't respond to a predator's advances, they go on to the next child. Simply put, blog sites are like road maps or blueprints for predators to effectively groom and/or seduce children.

This method of advertising by creating a blog is not a new phenomenon. Children and adults have been advertising themselves on the Internet for years. As a case in point, when you sign up for Internet service with America Online, you can have multiple screen names and can set up a profile for the screen name where personal information can be entered for all to see on the Internet. Children have been setting up profiles for years, some of which included photographs of themselves.

Law enforcement responses to online child exploitation are proactive and reactive. Posing on the Internet in an undercover capacity is an example of a proactive approach. Investigators pose as minors in areas of the Internet that tend to lure predators seeking young victims. For instance, chat rooms are popular with teenagers who are curious about sex and other related topics. The predator will attempt to contact minors in those types of chat rooms and then proceed to instant messaging (one to one) to begin the seduction process. The undercover investigator will seek out those types of chat rooms and wait to engage the predator in conversation. Once an online relationship is established, the predator typically attempts to discover everything about that child. This is done to try to reassure the child that it's all right to have positive feelings about having sex with adults. Predators have been known to send adult and child pornography to whom they believed was a child in order to lower the child's inhibitions.

Law enforcement investigators will occasionally pose as adults having similar interests as those of predators regarding sex with children. These types of investigations sometimes lead to the predator wanting to meet the undercover investigator who is posing as an adult who is willing to allow his or her own children to have sex with the predator or vice versa. This method has been effective in finding instances of unreported sex abuse of children.

3. LAW ENFORCEMENT'S RESPONSE

The reactive approach by law enforcement is generally due to citizen's complaints, referrals from other law enforcement agencies, or private organizations. Law enforcement agencies receive citizen's complaints daily, usually concerning spam (unsolicited e-mail) advertising child pornography Web sites. Other complaints can be a little more complicated. For example, a woman discovers a cache of child pornography on a home computer that she shares with her husband. The wife confides in her mother, another relative, or a friend, and that results in contact with law enforcement due to the fear that the children are at risk. This poses several issues for the investigator:

1. Will the wife cooperate?
2. What is her motive (impending divorce, child custody, etc.)?
3. Was the digital evidence properly preserved?
4. How many people had access to the computer?

5. Will the husband admit to the illegal activity and give permission to take the computer to be examined?
6. Was the computer compromised?

Investigators have to proceed carefully in this type of investigation and leave no stone unturned to successfully prove or disprove the allegation. Another example of a citizen's complaint is when a parent discovers their child has been receiving sexually explicit e-mail messages and pornography from an unknown person. Normally, the investigator would respond to the residence, interview the child and parents, and seize the computer to be examined at a computer forensic laboratory. If the child is cooperating and the predator is not aware of the discovery, the investigator can switch gears to a more proactive approach by assuming the child's online identity and continuing the e-mail and/or chats to see if the predator will arrange to meet.

Referrals from other law enforcement agencies occur quite often when the origi- nating agency does not have jurisdiction, experience in high-tech crimes, or does not have the resources to properly prosecute a person living in a different state. For instance, a local small police department in Florida receives a citizen's complaint that an unknown adult male living in Michigan solicited their 15-year-old daughter for sex while in a chat room. The police department investigators would have venue to pursue state charges but may lack financial resources to send investigators to Michigan for further investigation. They may also lack the knowledge and experience to conduct online investigations and preserve digital evidence. That investigator could provide the information to an Internet Crimes Against Children task force, if one is available in their area, contact the law enforcement agency in Michigan where the suspect resides, or contact the National Center for Missing and Exploited Children (NCMEC), which serves as a clearinghouse for complaints from citizens, law enforcement, and ISPs. NCMEC then would disseminate this information to the appropriate law enforcement agency for follow-up and investigation.

4. ONLINE FRAUDULENT THEFT CRIME

Crimes of this nature are primarily those committed with a computer, however, the computer in these instances is used as the "instrument" of the crime. Crimes such as credit card fraud and identity theft are two examples, and for purposes of this section, the focus will be on identity theft crime. One of the most common identity theft crimes involves "phishing," and it is defined as:

> The act of sending an e-mail to a user falsely claiming to be an established legitimate enterprise in an attempt to scam the user into surrendering private information that will be used for identity theft. The e-mail directs the user to visit a Web site where he/she is asked to update personal information, such as passwords, credit card, social security, and bank account numbers that any legitimate organization already would have had. The Web site, however, is bogus and set up only to steal the user's information. Phishing, also referred to as *brand spoofing* or *carding*, is a variation on "fishing," the idea being that bait is thrown out with the hopes that while most will ignore the bait, some will be tempted into biting *(6)*.

As previously discussed, most crimes committed on the Internet are not unique or new, but what is new is the contemporary method for which it is delivered. Phishing or scam type activities have been around for years, even predating the Internet. Through social engineering (social skills), criminals would use telephones and inside informants to gain valuable information from unsuspecting companies and or individuals.

An example of phishing occurred in 2003. Many eBay users received e-mails, supposedly from eBay, claiming that the user's account was about to be suspended unless they clicked on the provided link and updated their credit card information. Because it is relatively simple to make a Web site appear to be a legitimate organizations' site by mimicking the HTML code, the scam relied on the inherent trust that we, as human beings, possess. This culminated in tricking users into thinking they were actually being contacted by eBay to update their account information. By spamming large groups of people, the "phisher" counted on the e-mail being read by a percentage of people who actually had listed credit card numbers with eBay legitimately *(7)*.

Since 2003, there has been a significant increase in phishing scams. This increase has caused companies and individuals to suffer loss of money and/or stolen identity. Currently, there are private and government Web sites for companies and individuals who wish to report phishing scams. They also provide alerts for their subscribers concerning current threats and trends. For example, The Anti-Phishing Working Group (www.antiphishing.org) is a comprehensive site committed to wiping out Internet scams and fraud. Also, the Internet Crime Complaint Center (www.IC3.gov) was established to form a partnership between the FBI and National White Collar Crime Center (NW3C) to serve as a clearinghouse of reported incidents of fraud, computer intrusion, identity theft, and the growing list of Internet involved crimes.

Federal, state, and local law enforcement agencies have a difficult time investigating this type of criminal activity. The Federal Bureau of Investigation (FBI), U.S. Secret Service (USSS), and U.S. Postal Inspection Service (USPIS) have the personnel, expertise, and network of law enforcement contacts throughout the world to track down this type of criminal. According to Dan Larkin, Unit Chief at the FBI Internet Crime Complaint Center (IC3), "the Key to stopping phishers and bringing them to justice is to identify and target them quickly." Working in conjunction with antiphishing groups like "Digital Phishnet," Larkin further stated the need to "establish a pipeline directly to law enforcement, in real time, before the phisher has had time to disappear back into the anonymity of cyberspace" *(8)*.

5. COMPUTER INTRUSION

Cybercrimes such as network intrusion, hacking, virus distribution, denial of service attacks, hijacking (a computer or network), defacing Web sites, cyberstalking, and cyberterrorism are prevalent. In these instances, the computer itself becomes the "target" of the crime. Collectively they are all considered as computer intrusions.

5.1. Working Definition

A simple working definition of *computer intrusion* for investigators would be the following: "the unauthorized access of any computer system with the intent to cause system harm, steal information and/or hijack computer systems for further criminality." An important note here is the "unauthorized access" part of the definition. Some hackers indicate that they see nothing wrong with breaking into a computer system or network for the "challenge" of doing so, with no intent to do any damage. They are incorrect in their belief, as any unauthorized access to any computer system would be illegal.

5.2. *Legal Definition*

The legal definition of computer intrusion is defined differently in federal and state statutes. This is due to the multitude of crimes that are committed by unauthorized access of computer systems. For example, the federal statute that is commonly used in these offenses is titled "Fraud and related activity in connection with computers," which in part states:

(1) whoever having knowingly accessed a computer without authorization or exceeding authorized access, and by means of such conduct having obtained information that has been determined by the United States Government pursuant to an executive order or statute to require protection against unauthorized disclosure for reasons of national defense or foreign relations, or any restricted data, as defined in paragraph y of section 11 of the Atomic Energy Act of 1954, with reason to believe that such information so obtained could be used to the injury of the United States, or to the advantage of any foreign nation, willfully communicates, delivers, transmits, or causes to be communicated, delivered, or transmitted, or attempts to communicate, deliver, transmit or cause to be communicated, delivered, or transmitted the same to any person not entitled to receive it, or willfully retains the same and fails to deliver it to the officer or employee of the United States entitled to receive it;

(2) Intentionally accesses a computer without authorization or exceeds authorized access, and thereby obtains–

    (A) information contained in a financial record of a financial institution, or of a card issuer as defined in section 1602(n) of title 15, or contained in a file of a consumer reporting agency on a consumer, as such terms are defined in the Fair Credit Reporting Act (15 U.S.C. 1681 et seq.);

    (B) information from any department or agency of the United States; or

    (C) information from any protected computer if the conduct involved an interstate or foreign communication;

(3) intentionally, without authorization to access any nonpublic computer of a department or agency of the United States, accesses such a computer of that department or agency that is exclusively for the use of the Government of the United States or, in the case of a computer not exclusively for such use, is used by or for the Government of the United States and such conduct affects that use by or for the Government of the United States;

(4) knowingly and with intent to defraud, accesses a protected computer without authorization, or exceeds authorized access, and by means of such conduct furthers the intended fraud and obtains anything of value, unless the object of the fraud and the thing obtained consists only of the use of the computer and the value of such use is not more than $5,000 in any 1-year period;

(5) (A) (i) knowingly causes the transmission of a program, information, code, or command, and as a result of such conduct, intentionally causes damage without authorization, to a protected computer;

       (ii) intentionally accesses a protected computer without authorization, and as a result of such conduct, recklessly causes damage; or

    (iii) intentionally accesses a protected computer without authorization, and as a result of such conduct, causes damage; and

(B) by conduct described in clause (i), (ii), or (iii) of subparagraph (A), caused (or, in the case of an attempted offense, would, if completed, have caused)–

    (i) loss to 1 or more persons during any 1-year period (and, for purposes of an investigation, prosecution, or other proceeding brought by the United States only, loss resulting from a related course of conduct affecting 1 or more other protected computers) aggregating at least $5,000 in value;

    (ii) the modification or impairment, or potential modification or impairment, of the medical examination, diagnosis, treatment, or care of 1 or more individuals;

    (iii) physical injury to any person;

    (iv) a threat to public health or safety; or

    (v) damage affecting a computer system used by or for a government entity in furtherance of the administration of justice, national defense, or national security;

(6) knowingly and with intent to defraud traffics (as defined in section 1029) in any password or similar information through which a computer may be accessed without authorization, if–

(A) such trafficking affects interstate or foreign commerce; or

(B) such computer is used by or for the Government of the United States;

(7) with intent to extort from any person any money or other thing of value, transmits in interstate or foreign commerce any communication containing any threat to cause damage to a protected computer *(9)*.

An example of state law regarding computer intrusion can be seen in the following Florida law titled "Offenses against intellectual property," which in part states:

(1) Whoever willfully, knowingly, and without authorization modifies data, programs, or supporting documentation residing or existing internal or external to a computer, computer system, or computer network commits an offense against intellectual property.

(2) Whoever willfully, knowingly, and without authorization destroys data, programs, or supporting documentation residing or existing internal or external to a computer, computer system, or computer network commits an offense against intellectual property.

(3) (a) Data, programs, or supporting documentation which is a trade secret as defined in s. 812.081 which resides or exists internal or external to a computer, computer system, or computer network which is held by an agency as defined in chapter 119 is confidential and exempt from the provisions of s. 119.07*(1)* and s. 24(a), Art. I of the State Constitution.

    (b) Whoever willfully, knowingly, and without authorization discloses or takes data, programs, or supporting documentation which is a trade secret as defined in s. 812.081 or is confidential as provided by law residing or existing internal or external to a computer, computer system, or computer network commits an offense against intellectual property.

(4) (a) Except as otherwise provided in this subsection, an offense against intellectual
property is a felony of the third degree, punishable as provided in s. 775.082,
s. 775.083, or s. 775.084.

(b) If the offense is committed for the purpose of devising or executing any scheme
or artifice to defraud or to obtain any property, then the offender is guilty of a
felony of the second degree, punishable as provided in s. 775.082, s. 775.083,
or s. 775.084 *(10)*.

5.3. Law Enforcement's Response

In the early 1980s, hacking computers was a popular way for people with computer
knowledge to pull pranks. Some jargon files define a hacker as merely "a person
who enjoys exploring the details of programmable systems and how to stretch their
capabilities, as opposed to most users, who prefer to learn only the minimum necessary"
(11). Hollywood also began to glamorize hackers in movies, such as *War Games*,
Hackers, and *Net*, making these people underground heroes out to save the world from
evildoers.

This is not the case today in the cyberworld. Criminals and terrorists have realized
that remotely compromising the computer systems of government, industry, and educational institutions can be more beneficial and cause more havoc. The added advantage
is that they do not have to leave their secure surroundings nor put themselves at
risk of being detected or arrested. This is evident in the growing concerns by the
government and private entities that have made information security a priority in
everyday operation. Computer use policies and guidelines have been implemented in
the workplace and are strictly being enforced. Previously, because computer security
was not a priority, it also was not very well funded. Since then, the focus has changed,
and information security is now a top priority in both government and private industry.
The U.S. Computer Emergency Response Team (US-CERT) was created to coordinate
and facilitate cybersecurity information among government agencies. Established in
2003 to protect the nation's Internet infrastructure, US-CERT coordinates defense
against, and responses to, cyberattacks across the nation.

US-CERT is charged with protecting our nation's Internet infrastructure by coordinating
defense against, and response to cyberattacks. US-CERT is responsible for:

- analyzing and reducing cyberthreats and vulnerabilities
- disseminating cyberthreat warning information
- coordinating incident response activities

US-CERT interacts with federal agencies, industry, the research community, state and
local governments, and others to disseminate reasoned and actionable cybersecurity information to the public *(12)*.

The investigative response to an attack on a computer system is normally reactive.
The investigator usually receives a complaint of a particular incident and addresses it
appropriately based on the circumstances involved. For instance, if a network administrator discovers that unusual activity is occurring on the network and shuts down
the server, routers, and so forth, critical information may be lost if the routers are
not properly configured to save network traffic logs. When the network administrator restarts the network and discovers that data is being systematically deleted from

the server's database, he or she now knows or believes the computer network may have been compromised.

Law enforcement is contacted and responds to the scene. The investigators generally assess the situation to attempt to determine the intent of the intruder or intrusion. Presume in this case the hacker was malicious. Some possible suspects could include a former or current employee or an industrial competitor. The investigator would then make arrangements to have the system forensically analyzed by a forensic computer examiner. Afterward, the investigator would then meticulously review the evidence from the examination of the computer system. This usually consists of logs of the following: machine, history, message, system, firewall, router, and proxy servers. Some malicious programs that hackers may install on a victim's computer system are "Trojan" and "sniffer" programs. It is important that investigators look for these types of programs as they can assist in determining the method in which the intruder compromised the system.

The investigators typically work backwards from the point of attack to determine a timeline when the system may have been compromised. If the investigator identifies the method and location of the intrusion, certain traditional law enforcement techniques will come into play. Some examples are interviews, surveillance, legal process, search warrants, and so forth. A recent case publicized by the U.S. Department of Justice reflects the mentality of some individuals who are gaining access to computer networks with bad intentions:

> PATRICK ANGLE, age 34, currently of Columbus, Indiana, has been charged in a one-count Information with intentionally damaging a protected computer. The Information charges that ANGLE, who had worked for Varian, first in Gloucester and then from his home in Indiana, had become disgruntled with his employment by September, 2003, and had been told by the company that his contract would be terminated in October, 2003. It is alleged that to vent his frustration with Varian, on September 17, 2003, ANGLE logged into Varian's computer server in Massachusetts from his Indiana home and intentionally deleted the source code for the e-commerce software that he and others had been developing. He then covered his tracks by editing and deleting some of the computer logs of activity on the server and by changing the server's root password to make it difficult for other Varian employees to log on to the server and assess and repair the damage. The software source code that ANGLE deleted had been developed at great expense to Varian and would have been expensive to reproduce. Although Varian was ultimately able to recover the deleted material from backups, the recovery effort cost the company approximately $26,455. If convicted, ANGLE faces a maximum sentence of 10 years in prison, to be followed by 3 years of supervised release, a fine of up to $250,000, and restitution *(13)*.

6. CONCLUSION

As discussed in the above paragraphs, although cyberinvestigations are challenging, they can also be frustrating to an investigator. The areas of investigations have similar methods to identify cybercriminals, but the crimes themselves differ in the manner in which harm can be inflicted on society. The majority of the time, any damage done by a hacker who compromised a school's computer network and caused lost or altered data can be repaired or restored. However, the innocence of a child taken by an online predator is forever gone.

Individuals interested in becoming a cyberinvestigator should be prepared to attain formal education and experience in the computer technology field. The main attribute of a cyberinvestigator is solid old-fashioned police investigative skills. Having the ability to effectively interview and interrogate individuals is one good example. An investigator must seek out the facts to find the individual(s) responsible for the illicit activity. If an investigator is unable to effectively obtain information and/or admissions, it will prove extremely difficult in some situations to place a suspect behind the computer. It may then make it problematic to affect an arrest and/or prosecute individuals for their illegal acts. Cyberinvestigators should remember the person *behind* the computer committed the crime, not the *computer*.

REFERENCES

[1] Florida State Statute 827.071 (5).

[2] Claburn, T. (2006) "Study: Child Porn Isn't Illegal In Most Counteries" Available at http://www.information week. com/showArticle.jhtml;jsessionid=CQRJD44SELINQQSNDLOSKHSCJUNN2JVN?articleID=184429489& queryText=icmec.

[3] Hoover, JN. (2006) "Coalition Launched To Fight Child Pornography" Available at http://www.informationweek.com/ show Article.jhtml;jsessionid=CQRJD44SELINQQSNDLOSKHSCJUNN2JVN?articleID=183700705&query Text= richard+shelby.

[4] Title 18, United States Code, Section 2422(b).

[5] Florida State Statute 847.0135.

[6] Jupitermedia, "Phishing" Available at http://webopedia.com/TERM/p/phishing.html.

[7] Jupitermedia, "Phishing" Available at http://webopedia.com/TERM/p/phishing.html.

[8] Digitalriver, Inc, "Industry, Law Enforcement Team to Launch Digital PhishNet" http://www.digitalriver.com/ corporate/press_releases/pr_444.shtml.

[9] Title 18, USC, Section 1030.

[10] Florida State Statute 815.04.

[11] World Wide School "Hackers' Dictionary of Computer Jargon" May 1998 http://www.worldwideschool.org/ library/books/tech/computers/TheHackersDictionaryofComputerJargon/chap29.html.

[12] United States Computer Emergency Readiness Team (us-cert) http://www.us-cert.gov/aboutus.html.

[13] United States Department of Justice, "Former Employee Of A Massachusetts High-Technology Firm Charged With Computer Hacking" http://www.usdoj.gov/criminal/cybercrime/angleCharged.htm August 23, 2004.

Chapter 7

Duties, Support Functions, and Competencies: Digital Forensics Investigators

Larry R. Leibrock

Summary

If the digital forensics profession is to successfully meet both the current and emerging needs and duties inherent in our profession, we need to collaboratively develop, rigorously define, and collectively debate the tasks, practices, and competencies inherent in our investigative activities. The needs discussed in this chapter will serve to represent a consensus of the standards, emerging levels of professional practices, potential adversarial challenges, and development of acceptable levels of digital forensics investigation performance. As we work through this discussion, centering on the tasks, practices, and competencies, transparency of professional practice and better methodological rigor to our investigative work should also be included.

Key Words: Digital forensics, Digital forensics investigator, Forensic image, MD5, NIST, Operating systems, RAID.

1. DIGITAL FORENSICS INVESTIGATIONS OVERVIEW

Digital forensics investigations center typically on the examination of information and knowledge created, used, and stored on the physical media of a storage component of a digital device (termed *questioned device*; i.e., computer, digital camera, personal digital assistant). Typically speaking, this data is natively stored in binary format as ones and zeros. The investigator may also elect to determine the provenance of the questioned device.

From: *Handbook of Digital and Multimedia Forensic Evidence*
Edited by: J. J. Barbara © Humana Press Inc., Totowa, NJ

The basic digital forensics investigative process can be outlined as follows, however, the explicit use of controls and investigative protocols centers on procedural controls for the continuity of evidence and evidentiary extracts. This is necessary in order to have the absolute capacity to demonstrate linkages between the questioned device or system, evidentiary extracts, the investigative report, and the investigator's expert opinions. The generalized digital investigative framework includes:

1. Nonintrusive acquisition of a replicated image of data extracted from the questioned device. This is typically termed the *forensic image*.
2. Calculation of the authentication hash value necessary to properly authenticate the data stored on both the questioned device and the forensics image.
3. Conducting a file-fragment recovery procedure to "undelete" files, folders, and directory objects.
4. Performing a hash file signature analysis to note file attributes.
5. Recovering temp, swap, file slack, and page objects.
6. Searching for file hash values—known and unknown filters.
7. Searching for key-term strings.
8. Reviewing file notations.
9. Noting applications or indications of file manipulation activity such as file eradicators, encryption, file compressors, or file hiding utilities.
10. Reviewing typical evidentiary objects such as:

    A. Application software applications
    B. Digital camera, printer, and ancillary storage devices
    C. E-mails
    D. Games
    E. Graphics images
    F. Internet chat logs
    G. Latent data extraction from slack, page, temp, and registry spaces
    H. Network activity logs
    I. Recycle folders
    J. System and file date/time objects
    K. User-created directories, folders, and files

11. Preparing evidence summaries, exhibits, reports, and expert findings based on evidentiary extracts and investigative analysis.

2. ROLE OF DIGITAL FORENSICS INVESTIGATION TOOLS

As the digital forensics profession matures, more commercial investigative applications have been brought to market. The use of these tools has served to ease the tasks of investigators. However, these tools carry attending risks to inexperienced or unqualified investigators in that they may serve to isolate an investigator's understanding of the underlying digital investigative details of acquisition, hashes, analysis, and reporting.

The basic skills of digital investigation should not simply rely upon the automated scripts of any tool, but rather a competent investigator should understand the information technologies, basic investigative case theory, limitations of certain tools, and cross-validation techniques. The maturity of the digital forensics investigative profession must also not rely only on the use of tools; rather, the professional development should focus on models related to functions, specificity in certain duties, and emerging competencies. A discussion, conceptual listing, and critique of the general duties and supporting essential functions for a digital forensics investigator are a potentially fruitful level of discourse. The author envisions manifold values in collectively discussing digital forensics investigator duties, functions, and competencies.

3. DIGITAL FORENSICS INVESTIGATOR DUTIES, FUNCTIONS, AND COMPETENCIES

A significant value of this discourse is intended to represent a consensus of the professional standards, emerging levels of professional practices, potential adversarial challenges, and development of acceptable levels of digital forensics investigation performance. One should note that forensics investigator performance in our digital forensics practices is always at question, given our ethical, legal, and administrative responsibilities in the course of our professional investigative responsibilities and the litigious environment in which we must operate.

In this perspective, this chapter serves as a general competency model for the digital forensics investigator and the proper management of the digital forensics investigative unit. The general competency model is intended to reflect the prevailing forensics investigative life cycle (i.e., collection, examination, investigation, and reporting). Based on anecdotal observations, this investigative life cycle is the prevailing model in most digital forensics investigative activities. Obviously, in certain investigative settings or certain cases, either this aforementioned life cycle or this offered digital forensics investigator competency model may be modified as necessary to meet those case-unique environments or unit mission needs. The intent is not methodological rigidity; rather the proximate value is reasonable elicitation of general duties, functions, and competencies for the digital forensics investigator and the performance of professional digital forensics practices.

As an initial competency-focused effort and hopefully construed consensus-supported document, this chapter is intended to establish a set of:

1. General duties
2. Additional duties
3. Appropriate controls
4. Responsibilities

The purpose of these established constructs are to support the increasingly complex needs of a proficient and skilled professional forensics examiner in investigative settings. The goals are to utilize and introduce appropriate controls, reduce ambiguity, establish and validate proper work-flow standards, and produce consistently replicable, scientifically reliable results necessary for the conduct of a sufficient digital forensics investigation *(1)*.

The notion of sufficiency in forensics investigations is to conceive, properly conduct, and be capable of sustaining both competent peer and adversarial examinations before either an administrative review or before the trier of fact in trial settings. Finally, another potential value of this chapter is to serve for the inclusion of more robust quality controls and objective standards for elicitation of current and future duties, standards, and competencies for both the forensics investigator and the particular investigative unit. This will assist them in dealing with new missions, new requirements, and new information technologies, which will certainly continue to challenge our emerging and maturing profession.

3.1. General Duties

Under general supervision, the primary purpose of the digital forensics investigator (2) position is to work as an investigator functioning in a unit that is responsible for conducting the forensics examination of computers, digital media, and certain digital devices. Employees or designated contractors in this classification use controls, records, devices, computer equipment, instruments, and software in order to:

1. Collect
2. Examine
3. Investigate
4. Report

Information of investigative interest may be derived from questioned computers, devices, or media. The stepwise, controlled progression of collection, examination, investigation, and reports support both accuracy and efficiency in the use of resources, evidence, examiner time, forensics instruments, supportable observations, reliable findings, and expert opinions concerning users and usage of digital devices and information or data recorded therein.

The details of established procedures for the investigative life cycle—collection, examination, investigation, and reporting—would normally be specified in the investigative unit procedures guide (policies and procedures) that should be updated periodically. The digital forensics examiner has the overall responsibility for the forensics investigative life cycle and completion of the series of reports, typically in the form of interim or final investigative reports. The digital forensics investigator is responsible for overall maintenance of the investigative unit's safety, security, and proper operation of the digital investigation laboratory furnished equipment. The digital forensics investigator may also perform related investigative work as necessary and directed. One example of this "as necessary assigned work" would be crime-scene evidence-collection supporting activities.

3.2. Specific Duties and Responsibilities

The list of essential functions, as outlined herein, is intended to be representative of the tasks performed within a digital forensics investigator classification. The omission of any function does not preclude management from assigning duties not listed herein if such functions are a logical assignment to the position. Of note is the fact that any/all of these essential functions and competencies, with minor modification, can easily be incorporated into a unit's procedural guides (i.e., its policies and procedures):

1. **Collect either processed or unprocessed evidentiary systems items, evidence, or suspect property (i.e., intake, security, storage, chain of custody).** The investigator conducts a verification of the proper "bag and tag" procedures, and evidentiary marking requirements have been properly completed and are in accordance with unit controls. Digital investigators will make use of the unit or laboratory information management (LIMS) application system as appropriate.

2. **In certain situations, the requesting entity may provide a "statement of work" (SOW), which contains client needs, investigative requirements, issues, and investigative scope details.** The forensics examiner reviews the SOW, resolves ambiguities, and plans the necessary work accordingly. The SOW may contain constraints about data usage restrictions such as confidential, proprietary, and privileged requirements. The SOW, with any notes, is typically placed in the associated case file management or laboratory management application system in accord with the investigative unit procedures.

3. **Investigators must ensure that all evidence/property is properly marked, recorded, packaged, handled, stored, and warehoused in compliance with applicable regulations, statutes, associated quality standards, and appropriate investigative unit procedures.** Times and dates are verified using trusted time sources (radio-synchronized atomic clocks) recorded in GMT or local time settings. Markings will be unique and in accordance with laboratory requirements and control standards.

4. **Investigators must ensure all appropriate records, forms, and receipts are properly and correctly prepared and are contemporaneously completed.** Examples include, for instance, property receipts, loan forms, release forms, bench notes, case materials, and transfer forms. Chain of custody controls related to all phases of evidence controls are to be rigorously documented, recorded in practice, and anomalies noted and reported.

5. **When collecting and processing all items (evidence and property), investigators maintain awareness of and follow procedures for dealing with potential hazardous materials/waste in compliance with established statutes, regulations, and unit laboratory procedures.**

6. **During the collecting and processing of all evidentiary items, the investigator makes note of and reports any suspected trace evidence, clothing, hair, body fluids.** Subsequent to this notation, the unit that has particular trace evidence investigative responsibility should be promptly notified. Further, in most situations the digital examination should be terminated until trace evidence is evaluated by the appropriate trace evidence entity.

7. **Investigators ensure that all evidence records and related paperwork concerning evidence disposal/release/handling is accurate and complete**. This will be in accordance with statutes, quality standards, and investigative unit procedures. Also, investigators must maintain disposition records with various clients, investigative sponsors, investigative units, and law enforcement agencies as required.

8. **After completing all collection activities, the investigator ensures that the records are completed, factually correct, and have the necessary date/time and signature notations in accordance with quality controls and unit requirements.**

9. **Conduct the proper collection of the evidentiary system items, evidence, and suspect property.** The digital investigator should make note of physical characteristics, markings, anomalies, and serials of all items. A comparison of the known and suspect markings should be noted. The collection process is to be completed in accordance with the unit procedures, which include notations, uses of evidentiary photography, and removal of certain storage media and confirmation of actual and BIOS systems times. The characteristics of the evidentiary system (i.e., Computer/Processors, Systems Owner, Serial Numbers), types and number of disks, and ancillary devices should be noted. *Completion of all collection activities is necessary before initiation of any examination procedures.*

10. **After completion of the collection procedures, the digital forensics investigator conducts the nonintrusive sector-by-sector copy (extraction) of the physical storage device using unit procedures.** The unit procedures will specify the disk extraction utility program and validated version (i.e., dd, DCFLD-dd, Encase®, SafeBack®). Extraction is typically done on forensically sterile media as specified in the unit procedures. The forensics data extraction is always performed in accordance with the unit procedures and standardized hash verification (message digests) records are noted and properly recorded (i.e., MD5, SHA1, or SHA256). The examiner must understand the concepts of data and file state, one-way hashing tool, and hash signature (message digest). The use of the selected variant of the verification hash is specified in the unit procedures. On a periodic basis, hash software tools verification and newly released versions should be tested, verified, and documented prior to use in digital forensics production activities. The calibration and verification test suite is typically documented in accordance with laboratory procedures and quality.

11. **The use of all associated hardware device write blockers must be verified as to their read-only functions before the initiation of the nonintrusive extraction.** The number of extracted copies is normally described in unit procedures. In some cases, multiple extractions must result in independent copies uniquely numbered. All copies must have identical hash verification values and verified hash creation date/time values. In certain cases, a copy may be subsequently placed in locked storage. This copy is an exemplar and typically no further forensics process is used on this copy.

12. **The working copy, which contains the extracted data, is encapsulated by the investigator into the unique case record file and stored using the validated version of the software forensics instrument (i.e., WinHex®, ProDiscover®, Forensics Tool Kit®, Encase®, or SMART®).** The case record file is then stored on a secured examination server *(3)*. Prior to this, the investigator must already have verified that the server is not connected to the open Internet, that it has the latest virus/malicious software and has been checked, and all user access controls have been properly enabled and verified to be operational at the time of the examination. *Completion of all these activities is necessary before initiation of any investigation procedures.*

13. **At the initiation of the investigation, the forensics investigator notes the suspect operating system, presence and characterization of extant file partitions, and file systems with the notable logical organization of the digital media.** The examiner notes presence of allocated, unallocated, and file fragments contained within the extracted data. The examiner must be able to recognize, note, and explain the distinctions among the logical constructs of files; allocated, unallocated, file fragments, slack, and overwritten. The examiner must understand and be able to explain the concepts of partition; file indexing, file, sector, and cluster. The investigator again confirms the comparisons of the hash verification values for the forensics extracts. The extent of notations is specified in the unit procedures guide that supports the digital forensics investigation.

14. **The digital forensics investigator operates the secured and restricted access examination server system to conduct folder/file un-deletion on the extracted data sets.** This action is done for the complete logical structure contained on the forensics extract of the media.

15. **The digital forensics investigator operates the secured and restricted access examination server system to conduct file signature analysis mismatch on the extracted data sets using known file signatures for comparison of file characteristics.** The unit may elect to use and maintain the current file hash compilation data set (i.e., NIST

Hash File Sets). The presence of mismatched files will be noted. The extent of notations is specified in the unit procedures guide that supports the digital forensics examination.

16. **The digital forensics investigator operates the examination server system to conduct key-term occurrences and forensics filtering on the extracted data sets.** The extent of notations is specified in the unit procedures guide that supports the digital forensics examination.

17. **The digital forensics investigator operates the examination server system to conduct application characterization of any suspected data eradication or data-altering activities.** The extent of notations is specified in the unit procedures guide that supports the digital forensics examination. *Completion of all investigation activities is necessary before reporting procedures.*

18. **The digital forensics investigator's reporting procedures necessitate the development of the basis of expert observations, findings, and opinions.** The investigator should continuously focus on the explicit basis for all evidence-based notations, investigative findings, and opinions. The correct characterization of the basis of findings and opinions are central to the investigative reporting process. The basis, findings, and opinions are noted and integrated into the unit or laboratory report forms. The investigator may utilize various techniques to selectively cross-validate some findings to serve as a risk management, quality verification approach. The use of these cross-validation techniques will be noted in the laboratory investigative report. The extent of cross-validation procedures may be specified in the unit procedures guide that supports the digital forensics examination. The use of cross-validation techniques should be central to the individual examiner's discretion on a case-specific basis.

19. **The digital forensics investigator typically prepares the contemporaneous bench notes and the interim or final reports that contain the notations, basis, findings, and opinions of the particular investigation.** All notes and reports will be in the standard form in accord with unit procedures. The comparison of hash values is noted at the conclusion of the reporting process. Evidence files contained on the server evidentiary copy and all work copies are compared with the noted original hash value in order to ensure nonintrusive investigative techniques and noncontamination of the evidentiary copy. The investigator then ensures that the laboratory investigative report has both the necessary date/time and proper signature or reviewer notations.

20. **The digital forensics investigator may review the particular case file, procedures, notes, and reports with a designated peer or supervising examiner.** All concerns, conflicts, or differences are noted and, if necessary, subsequently presented for unit review among investigative unit peers and management. The extent of laboratory investigative report review procedures notations are specified in the unit procedures guide that supports the digital forensics examination.

21. **The digital forensics investigator will contemporaneously document actions and procedures when dealing with unexpected material; any unusual or anomalous evidentiary and investigative situations as they are encountered during collection, examination, analysis, or reporting procedures.** These documented actions and procedures will be recorded and reported to peers and managers.

22. **The digital forensics investigator, who encounters any accuracy concerns, need for revised or potentially new processes, procedures, or potential quality issues, should feel free to exercise an "open door" review with any unit worker, quality manager, or appropriate supervisor.**

23. **The digital forensics investigator periodically reads the unit procedures guides, technical notices, unit workflow changes, and forensics tool qualifications.** The examiner ensures currency and congruence in the use of validated version updates and ensures forensics work is in accord and fully complies with the current unit procedures guide and appropriate documentation. The investigator maintains appropriate records and documents in accordance with unit records policies and properly destroys nonretained records, work materials, and notes.

24. **The digital forensics investigator observes for and reports to management any potential information as to actual or potential conflicts that deal with particular situations, cases, previous relationships, or potential sources that could compromise any disinterested investigator relationships.**

25. **The digital forensics investigator meets with unit personnel for technical tool qualifications, procedure reviews, organizational development, laboratory safety, and quality meetings.**

26. **The digital forensics investigator participates in professional development through reviews, technical workshops, and continuing education programs.**

Management should review their defined essential functions and incorporate those from this listing that are not currently specified in the unit procedures guide that supports the digital forensics examination. Additional essential functions may be identified by management based on departmental policies and procedures.

3.3. *Additional Functions*

Although the following tasks are necessary for the work of the forensics investigative unit, they are not an essential part of the purpose of the digital forensics examiner position. These functions are not performed by those investigators with limited forensics knowledge and experience.

The digital forensics investigator will perform additional related duties as directed:

1. **The digital forensics investigator may perform liaison, communications, notifications, and documentary requirements with crime scene personnel, investigative officers, evidentiary property discovery, pick-up and safe transport from various locations.**

2. **The digital forensics investigator may be asked to conduct additional time and work estimates when requested for planning digital forensics investigations.**

3. **The digital forensics investigator may be tasked to prepare screen captures, identification and comparison exhibits, log collections, and graphical representations for investigative, depositional, and for quality review purposes.**

4. **The investigator may be tasked with conducting installed application listings contained on evidentiary images.**

5. **The investigator may be tasked with determining the presence and characterization of adult sexual images or the presence and characterization of minor sexual images (contraband) contained on evidentiary images.**

6. **In specific instances, the digital forensics investigator may be tasked with conducting an investigation or "breaking" of cryptographic or steganographic instances contained on evidentiary images.**

7. **In specific instances, the digital forensics investigator may be tasked with conducting an investigation of characterization for specified software applications and code segments.**

8. The digital forensics investigator may be tasked with performing image characterization and enhancements on certain type of imagery.
9. The digital forensics investigator may be tasked to observe the presence of proprietary or trade-secret business records in the evidentiary materials.
10. The digital forensics investigator may be tasked to perform extractions and placing in reviewable stores certain composite files of investigative data (i.e., e-mail archives, digital imagery, Web logs, and networking files).
11. The digital forensics investigator may be tasked to search for and characterize the presence of ancillary or complementary data storage or archival devices and associated media.
12. The digital forensics investigator may be tasked to perform Internet-based Web searches and network traces for evidence (to support or corroborate information or refute certain findings, opinions, suppositions, or allegations).
13. The digital forensics investigator may be tasked with determining the versions of all installed operating systems, presence of virtual environments, user accounts, and last usage times.
14. The digital forensics investigator may be tasked with locating metadata associated with office productivity data contained in the evidentiary image.
15. The digital forensics investigator may be tasked to conduct forensics analysis of differing types of optical storage media (i.e., CD or DVD).
16. The digital forensics investigator may be tasked to conduct forensics analysis of magnetic storage media (i.e., tape media, USB disk storage, Firewire disk storage, ZIP® drives, removable diskette, and removable disk drives).
17. The digital forensics investigator may be tasked to conduct a forensics analysis of a cellular telephone and its uses.
18. The digital forensics investigator may be tasked to conduct a forensics analysis of a personal digital assistant (i.e., Palm Pilot®, Windows CE®, and Blackberry®) and its uses.
19. The digital forensics investigator may be tasked to conduct a forensics analysis of digital cameras and their images.
20. The digital forensics investigator may be tasked to conduct an extraction of a digitally encoded audio file for subsequent audio analysis.
21. The digital forensics investigator may be tasked to conduct Redundant Array of Inexpensive Disks (RAID) or Storage Area Network (SAN) data repository server data acquisition/extraction and investigations (which involve the server and data stores).
22. The digital forensics investigator may be tasked to conduct a peer-to-peer data acquisition/extraction and investigation.
23. The digital forensics investigator may be tasked to conduct an indexing of allocated data contained on media or systems.
24. The digital forensics investigator may be tasked to create data models, data mining, and data warehouses for investigation of data repositories.
25. The digital forensics investigator may be tasked to conduct a live memory data acquisition.
26. The digital forensics investigator may be tasked to develop revised or experimental test procedures and test guidelines for nonproduction use in certain digital forensics tasks.
27. The digital forensics investigator may be tasked to perform individual training and technical demonstrations as needed or requested.

28. The digital forensics investigator may be tasked with maintaining records and logs for the forensics system and performing the archiving of all original and enhanced images.

29. The digital forensics investigator may be required to obtain, sign, and use Pretty Good Protection (PGP) or X.509 certificates in the investigative forensics life cycle.

30. The digital forensics investigator may be tasked to compile and calculate various types of statistics from logs and other unit records information.

31. The digital forensics investigator may be tasked to analyze and evaluate evidence for further enhancement and make recommendations for the proper conditions necessary for optimal forensics enhancement and further production.

32. The digital forensics investigator may be tasked with comparison, validation, and reliability testing for new tools, new releases, and standard scripting.

33. The digital forensics investigator may be tasked with standardizing sample directory structures for organizing work on the investigative server.

34. The digital forensics investigator may be tasked with communicating with clients or investigators regarding their investigative requests and communicating with outside entities and agencies involved in digital forensics functions and requirements.

35. The digital forensics investigator may be tasked with preparing materials, reports, demonstrations, and presentations for interrogatories, depositions, court purposes, and trials.

36. The digital forensics examiner may have to testify in courts of law as directed or when so subpoenaed.

37. The digital forensics investigator may have to defend the given investigative protocol, extant procedures, forensics instruments, report, opinions, and findings before a trier-of-fact.

38. The digital forensics investigator may have to provide technically and legally sufficient definitions to prevailing forensics terms of art.

39. The digital forensics investigator may be tasked to evaluate other forensics examiners work and at-court testimony activities delivered by other examiners.

40. The digital forensics investigator may be tasked to participate in a "red-team" review of complex forensics reports in preparation for jury delivery and adversarial review.

41. The digital forensics investigator may be tasked to forensically eradicate the original evidence, work records, extracts, or case files. Eradication of forensics data and records is initiated only upon receipt of appropriate and legally sufficient directive. Digital eradication is done using verified and validated software tools (i.e., Winhex© or BC Wipe®). In certain jurisdictions, the digital forensics investigator may be required to produce a witnessed certificate of destruction.

42. The digital forensics investigator may be tasked with performing systems maintenance on equipment.

43. The digital forensics investigator may be tasked to support, validate, test, or provide input into change management tools, version testing and procedures for information systems, case management systems, and laboratory document control systems. This serves to support the disciplined testing, release approval, and retirement processes.

44. The digital forensics investigator may be tasked to conduct research on new techniques, methodologies, and procedures (applies to work under charge).

45. The digital forensics investigator may be tasked with providing his or her supervisor with recommendations concerning upgrades or new equipment requirements as appropriate.

46. The digital forensics investigator may be tasked with keeping his or her professional qualifications, relevant case experience, and testifying history updated for expert qualifications.

47. The digital forensics investigator may be tasked with being an ex-partite expert in the role of technical expert, special master, or arbitration resource in litigation or disputes.

48. The digital forensics investigator may be tasked with maintaining a library of useful documents, data repositories, investigative manuals, texts, and Web references.

49. The digital forensics investigator may be assigned responsibility to maintain software tools that may include license management, source drive management, and forensics instruments repositories for the unit's use.

50. The digital forensics investigator may request or be required to attend new technology training and orientation as the requirements, new information technologies, and client needs arise.

51. The digital forensics investigator may be tasked with working in interdisciplinary investigative or legal teams to help resolve discovery evidentiary issues in certain complex matters.

52. The digital forensics investigator may be requested to provide input into quality control procedures and standards with efficacy to the particular digital forensics practices (i.e., International Standards Organization (ISO) and particular laboratory procedures).

53. The digital forensics investigator may be tasked with working on American Society of Criminal Lab Directors/Laboratory Accreditation Board (ASCLD/LAB) procedures or standards development and accreditation activities (see Chapter 3).

As can be ascertained from the above listings, there are a considerable number of ancillary functions that can be applicable to the digital forensics investigator. Depending upon management's needs, some may become essential functions. For example, management's decision to have its digital forensics unit attain accreditation by ASCLD/LAB will automatically require many of the ancillary functions to become essential functions.

4. MINIMUM TRAINING AND EXPERIENCE

Regarding training and experience, a new digital forensics investigator should minimally have obtained his or her baccalaureate degree. This should be supplemented by at least one year of progressively knowledgeable and skilled experience in digital forensics examinations and investigations. Preferably, this skilled experience is obtained in an intelligence collection, law enforcement, or criminal justice environment. Conversely, an equivalent combination of education, training, and/or experience may suffice. This is often determined by the needs of the hiring agency. For those individuals wishing to work for local, state, or federal law enforcement agencies, police records checks, financial records check, military service records, personal background, and drug testing will normally be required as a condition of employment.

All digital forensics investigators must complete a minimum of 40 hours of introductory digital forensics training, which includes the successful completion of a testing component (i.e., practical examination, written test, oral test, etc.). Employed digital forensics investigators must complete a minimum of 16 hours of either standardization or proficiency digital forensics training on an annual basis. In certain jurisdictions, proper licensure as a member of law enforcement, designated forensics examiner, or private investigator is mandatory (see Chapter 2).

NOTES

1. The specification of procedures will be found in the unit's procedural guides, not in this model duty, support functions, and competencies chapter.
2. The concept *employee* means a full-time or part-time person serving in an employee or contractor status.
3. The term *server* means a forensics examiner–controlled computational system with associated investigative software, instruments, access/usage logging, and protective access mechanisms expressly utilized for forensics investigative activities. The server typically has case partitioned with appropriate level of evidentiary and case-related data access controls.

Chapter 8

Electronic Evidence and Digital Forensics Testimony in Court

Fred Chris Smith and Erin E. Kenneally

Summary

Like many of the chapters in this book, this chapter will succeed to the extent that it is able to raise many more questions than it can answer. Because of the constantly changing nature of the contemporary standards for the admission of highly technical digital forensic expert witness testimony, our subject matter is a fast-moving target. What is essential for the tyro who is interested in learning how to testify and how best to present clear and cogent testimony about complex technological issues, processes, or investigations is to develop a scientific attitude about every aspect of his or her forensic work. That attitude must be maintained without becoming overly concerned with the clear differences between evolving standards to ascertain the nature of digital forensics expertise and the long-standing traditions for providing provenance for experts in the hard sciences such as physics or chemistry.

Key Words: *Daubert*, Electronic evidence, Exculpatory, FRE 702, Inculpatory, Information security, *Kumho Tire*.

1. NEW ROLES FOR INFORMATION TECHNOLOGY EXPERTS: JURIES

Today, many of us find ourselves living ever increasing aspects of our lives in a virtual, electronic world, simultaneously existing in different time zones while working, playing, and communicating instantly across geographic borders. Copies and bits and pieces of the electronic artifacts and records created by our networked activities can be found or may ultimately be stored in an almost infinite number of forms and places. People who use telecommunications technologies in their daily undertakings, especially those who are concerned about privacy issues, are beginning to have at least a basic

From: *Handbook of Digital and Multimedia Forensic Evidence*
Edited by: J. J. Barbara © Humana Press Inc., Totowa, NJ

understanding that once created, the isolation and security of electronic information, and its electronic trail of evidence, is a difficult thing to achieve.

Average consumers of telecommunication and other information technologies are beginning to understand that the systems that provide these services are extremely complex and subject to various kinds of failures from time to time. However, few of the countless consumers of these increasingly essential services or even the more sophisticated and avid users of information technologies fully appreciate the amount of potential electronic evidence that is created with the normal use of a networked computer, a wireless laptop, or a Blackberry or other cellular device, and that can be preserved, manipulated, lost, or rediscovered at some future time through forensic techniques. These individuals and others with no computer experience whatsoever, and everything in between these extremes, combine from time to time to compose a jury of one's peers and the audiences for technical expert witness testimony.

Enter the information technology (IT) expert. Many of the recognized areas of IT and digital forensics still lack the kinds of integrated academic programs of higher education or any long-standing traditions of certification and licensing necessary for "experts" to practice their crafts. Generally, an IT expert is not subjected to examination, criticism, or even disqualification by official arms of their professional communities of interest. So, when IT forensic experts are required to answer difficult questions about digital evidence at a hearing or trial before a particular judge or jury, each case can become a new precedent for the consideration of the peers of the testifying expert.

1.1. *"Electrification of Evidence"*

Because of the growing importance of digital evidence to the system of justice and its increased use in the resolution of crucial issues in a large and growing number of legal conflicts, it has become incumbent on the trial bar to seek out IT technical experts. The other side of that coin is the growing pressure on the IT industry to produce competent experts to assist lawyers for the parties and the courts in the preparation and trial of cases that involve complicated issues that arise out of the need to introduce electronic evidence. Lacking the sorts of indices that lawyers, judges, and jurors have come to rely upon in determining which of the competing experts is the most competent and therefore the most credible in their testimony at trial, the IT community has struggled with ways to come up with adequate assurances of expertise. Standards for the admission of evidence of all kinds have evolved over a century or two of trial-and-error to assure the fact finder that the expertise being offered is reliable and that the expert has the knowledge, experience, and training, even though these may have been acquired outside the traditionally recognized educational, economic, and political institutional structures.

1.2. *Judges*

This chapter explains the way the courts have applied the evolving judicial standards for overseeing the qualification of IT technical experts and determining the reliability of their findings and the admissibility of their opinions. Technical experts often testify as merely factual witnesses, and like many other factual witnesses, they may use technical means to assist them in presenting their testimony. Almost any witness can improve his or her ability to communicate information and to prepare interesting reports, whether or not they are being called as a witness to render an expert opinion about an issue in a lawsuit. Accordingly, a technical expert who believes he or she will be called or who is interested in being called as a witness can and should avail themselves of the wealth of literature and other forms of training and educational aides to become a better communicator.

This is not a trivial issue for technically skilled individuals who may have little or no public speaking experience. Individuals who are involved in one way or another in handling digital information that may prove to be relevant evidence in a civil or criminal case are as likely as not to end up on the witness stand, whether they affirmatively seek the experience as expert witnesses or not. As Bill Gates found out, much to his chagrin in the Microsoft civil antitrust case, no one—no matter how rich or famous—is immune from being subpoenaed as a witness and forced to give a deposition or to testify at a hearing or trial before a judge or jury and be cross-examined by a lawyer who seldom will have the examinee's best interests in mind.

1.3. Trials

The following abbreviated overview of the history of trial by jury in the United States and the increasing use of expert witnesses by lawyers to help present their cases focuses on criminal litigation. There are also an increasing number of civil cases, primarily dealing with the discovery of electronic evidence, that the reader should bear in mind, such as the landmark case for our purposes, *Gates Rubber Co. v. Bando Chemical Industries* (167 Federal Rules Decisions, p. 90; decided by a Colorado Federal District Court in 1996), which will be discussed later in this chapter.

1.4. Cases

It is quite likely that decisions dealing with digital forensic issues will soon be equally spread between civil and criminal litigation. For those primarily interested in tracking the developing civil case law, an excellent start is the supplement to the *Massachusetts Expert Witnesses*, *Volume I*, Chapter 11, entitled "Digital Discovery," published by Massachusetts Continuing Legal Education, Inc., in 2004. It is also available online through Lexis and Westlaw services. That article addresses both the case law and practice points for computer forensics experts who are engaged in electronic discovery in civil litigation and is written by a recognized electronic evidence expert, John H. Jessen, and three experienced attorneys, Charles R. Kellner, Paul M. Tobertson, and Lawrence T. Stanley.

Any dedicated expert should develop a source for legal decisions in order to keep abreast of new rulings on the qualification of forensic experts in general and for admitting expert opinions about electronic evidence, especially in the state and federal jurisdictions where the expert plans to testify. Many new books, guides, and free online resources have appeared for those involved with criminal litigation, such as the U.S. Department of Justice Computer Crime and Intellectual Property Section Web site at http://www.cybercrime.gov/. It contains an excellent treatise that is constantly updated on the search and seizure of computers, together with summaries of the federal computer crime cases that have been brought or are currently pending. The National Institute of Justice has published a series of guides for state and local law enforcement covering the various stages of computer crime investigation. One of the authors has contributed to the most recently compiled volume, entitled *Electronic Evidence in the Courtroom*, Which is be published in 2007, and is be available online free of charge at http://www.ojp.usdoj.gov/nij/.

2. THE MARKET DEMAND FOR IT EXPERTS (1)

During legal disputes, investigators (systems administrators, forensic examiners, regulators, private and public law enforcement) will often rely on digital evidence in the form of audit and transaction logs and system and network artifacts to prove/disprove their claims. Digital logs can contain virtually any type of data that a computer system is programmed to capture, including transactional events, content, and communications between and among human operators and the machines with which they interface. This includes anything from network activity captured by intrusion detection systems or firewalls (including any monitoring tool that logs data such as tcp dump, snort, sendmail, syslog, Web servers, backup clients, e-mail server, etc.), to e-mail messages and user account records, to system level syslog or kernel activity (2).

IT experts will increasingly be called upon due to the fact that information assurance and the ability to maintain the integrity of digital data for the purposes of legal proof is continually challenged by the nature of network computing, system bugs and vulnerabilities, and constantly changing technology. These features have conspired to create confusion surrounding the way traditional rules and standards are applied to the admissibility of digital evidence.

What is the default posture that courts have taken thus far toward digital evidence reliability? Does it make sense to afford electronic evidence produced by computers any presumption of reliability unless and until it is challenged by the opposing party or proven to be untrustworthy? Or, because of the increasing number of questions concerning information authenticity assurances, should digital artifacts be presumed unreliable until guarantees of trustworthiness are shown? Should there be any presumption one way or the other? If not, what are the reliability controls that courts should demand in order to keep litigation from taking over the other issues in a case? For instance, should an e-mail or log be denied admissibility because it was retrieved from a database that was unsecured and subject to tampering? Or, should the party disputing the transaction that the digital evidence is offered as proof have to show actual penetration and alteration of the log data? In light of these and many other questions concerning the applicable evidentiary standards and presumptions, IT experts are going to be called upon by the courts to raise or lower the bar for successful challenges to the integrity of digital evidence by testifying to the truth of the matter based on their specialized knowledge of information technology, applied in highly fact specific contexts.

This reliance on IT experts will be driven by the need to facilitate a just legal framework for establishing the trustworthiness of the reconstructed realities in litigation that are increasingly based on digital artifacts and in recognition of the fundamental uncertainties in the processes involved in utilizing these artifacts as evidence. These forensic uncertainties are not being adequately addressed by current information assurance practices and product development processes (i.e., many IT corporate and government departments lack meaningful guidance on how to implement IT to bolster digital information reliability), and these uncertainties risk being perpetuated if the operative assumptions underlying legal interpretations of the industry reliability standards are institutionalized by the courts without first requiring proper measurement policies, procedures, and testing standards. The likely implications of institutionalizing on the current foundations are inefficient dispute resolution and escalating embarrassment for experts who are required to sort through these problems under oath *(3)*.

This chapter posits that the digital environment challenges our interpretation and measurement of trustworthy evidence and that the key to assuring the reliability of the truth painted in litigation lies with the IT expert.

2.1. Data Digitization and Automation: Transactions Sans Humans

The ubiquity of computing in the current information age is manifest in essentially every aspect of our lives and has led experts to predict that in the near future, almost everything that humans and computers do will be observed and recorded. Furthermore, these records will be in demand by persons who might benefit from proving the past *(4)*. This is reinforced by studies that quantify the diminishing role that paper and printed documents are playing in the business world. The growth in digitization will likely continue to flourish given how data storage capacity continues to expand exponentially in parallel with plummeting costs *(5)*.

Digital evidence is significant because it is increasingly relied upon by trial lawyers to represent facts and to prove transactions. Rather than resulting from direct interactions between human authors and physical media (i.e., paper documents, books, letters), these facts and transactions exist digitally as a product of human interaction with computers and various automated acts carried out between computers. Experts most often attempt to trace back the electronic evidence trail to a relevant human actor. Digital evidence is the manifestation of temporal and spatial features of human–machine and machine–machine transactions. To explain, if transactions are "the doing or performing of any business, the management of any affair; or performance," then digital artifacts are evidence of these transactions. These transactions range across a myriad of business processes such as sales and purchases; contracts; sales, marketing, personnel, planning, and governance decisions; intruders trying to access computer systems; user account activity; and amounts of e-mail communications *(6)*.

In addition to the ubiquity of data digitization, the proliferation of computer automation increases the prevalence of digital evidence. Advances in IT have fostered the evolution of automated business processes whereby manual tasks are being minimized and eliminated for the purpose of increasing economy, efficiency, and effectiveness. In other words, variables such as time, distance, and human cognition are manipulated to facilitate business productivity. This is an environment where paper records and disjointed electronic data systems are being replaced by unbroken electronic streams of information connecting people and technologies used in previously unconnected transaction record-keeping.

Automated transactions have become so omnipresent as to be unnoticeable. The "AutoSpellCheck-&-Correct" feature in word-processing programs is a simple example of off-loading onto computers the manual processes of finding and replacing misspelled words—no human action or intention is necessary or inferable. Other more complicated and consequential examples of automation include the process of patient drug dispersal in the health care industry and STP (straight-through processing) in the securities industry. The former process minimizes the number of persons and the documentation involved in the administration of medication, and the latter removes manual processes in the trade-processing cycle between broker and clearinghouse *(7)*. To be sure, the litany of automated processes that are performed by computers is lengthy and well-known; they are mentioned here to underscore the implications for legally admissible proof when computers increasingly replace manual human processes. For example, evolving technologies such as Web services are automating transactions between business partners so that everything from ordering supplies, fulfillment, billing, and inventory management will no longer be disconnected nor require human interaction or real-time auditing along each step in the process *(8)*.

The consequence of all this is that IT experts are needed to interpret events and transactions occurring sans human involvement. IT expert testimony is becoming the mouthpiece through which triers of fact come to understand the nature and significance of transactions that occur between computers, an exchange that often occurs without direct human involvement. As such, dispute resolution surrounding automated, electronic transactions is dependent on how IT experts reconstruct reality during litigation based on their discretionary application of reliability principles to the relevant facts of a case.

For example, Internet-enabled business-to-business (B2B) e-commerce involves applying traditional paper-based transactions to online exchanges with partners *(9)*. However, the same business rules that guide these processes are now automated, so requirements such as secure messaging and delivery, authentication of buyers, and bank-approved spending limits are conducted without manual review and human interdiction. Ensuring the nonrepudiation of orders and guaranteeing the receipt of transactions is done via technologies such as public key infrastructure (PKI), which uses digital certificates and signatures. Given the migration of business transactions to computer-based interactions *(10)*, fraud from customers, business partners, and other insider abuse are making the transition as well *(11)*. So, proving the "who, what, when, where, and how" of a disputed funds transfer in this automated environment implicates the electronic records that have supplanted real-time human controls.

Although automation may usher in a new form of evidence relevant to dispute resolution, the conservative nature of the justice system has attempted to apply the traditional, underlying principles of proof in ways that are strikingly similar to those that have evolved to screen evidence based on physical-world concepts. Accordingly, Locard's Principle (that every contact leaves a trace) remains the foundational construct underlying the new practices of digital forensic identification. There is intuitive appeal to holding that a cross-transfer of evidence occurs whenever a person or a computer comes into contact with an object such that associations can be made between persons, locations, items, and actions in the real and virtual worlds *(12)*. Detecting and documenting this exchange means that persons (including cybercriminals) can be associated with locations, victims, items of evidence, and specific actions. IT experts have attempted to adapt this "cross-transfer" of evidence between and among computers and humans, whether it is to trace back and track down digital miscreants for law enforcement purposes or to prove-up business processes. IT experts have most often attempted to conform their findings to the process of identifying and presenting this evidentiary exchange between the human and technology objects that come into contact.

The growth of electronic discovery is a compelling illustration of how information digitization and automation is making new demands on IT experts. Information is the target in legal discovery. Consequently, IT experts figure prominently in assuring that electronic data and the processes used to create, manage, and store it are reliable and responsive. Traditional back-up schemes and copying onto digital media leave open the opportunity to challenge the data integrity; that is, completeness and accuracy is often unverified or data may not be easily accessible due to legacy equipment (hardware and software) or data management challenges. IT experts are called upon to introduce assurances of data integrity to digital discovery processes that are easily wrought with mistaken assumptions or fraud. Claims of spoliation are exacerbated by virtue of the fact that normal computer usage may alter data related to file access/modification/deletion, leaving open unresolved doubts about fraudulent activity and information integrity.

2.2. IT Experts and Implicit Challenges to Evidence: Electronic Ignorance Is Not Bliss

Willful blindness to the existence of electronic data and claimed ignorance of its susceptibility to alteration will no longer suffice. Due diligence in our digital society means that there is an affirmative duty to use reasonable care to collect, transmit, and securely store electronic data *(13)*. IT expert testimony can be used as either a sword or shield to confirm or disprove an allegation of wrongdoing. To be sure, handling a traditional hostile work claim might call for an employer to rectify the activity creating a hostile environment by enforcing policies and procedures that address sexual harassment (i.e., confront the harassing person and ensure that the activity ceases). But resolving ensuing litigation would involve human-to-human accounts of what was said and/or done, backed by various electronic sources of evidence. True, the situation could boil down to familiar he-said/she-said proofs, but in the context of the electronic medium, it becomes much easier to use and abuse technology as a less transparent basis for false-positive evidence and inferences to support opposing arguments *(14)*.

The information vulnerabilities wrought by Internet-worked computer–human exchanges involve another layer of technology controls that can only be interpolated by persons skilled in understanding how to re-create human-computer activities. The probability of fabrication is higher because the enabling "tools" are available to more employees and to others; the recidivism rate is greater because the technical enablers are indiscriminate (in the absence of some advance that would allow detection, computers are not affected by social norms or sensitization that may deter humans from engaging in harassing behavior); and these capabilities are a feature of any Peer to Peer (P2P) technology, regardless of the corporate environment.

2.3. InfoSec, Data Vulnerability, and Implications for the Truth

It is beyond the scope of this chapter to analyze the plethora of threats to information exacerbated by vulnerabilities in hardware, software, and network interfaces in conjunction with malicious attacks and other threats *(15)*. All of these occurrences serve as a reminder that the Internet is not secure; the interfaces between computers and networks enable these security threats to propagate; and security vulnerabilities affect individual computers connected to the Internet and the data that is stored or that passes between them *(16)*.

Information security is not a black-and-white event but rather a chain of hardware, software, networks, and human components that is only as strong as its weakest link *(17)*. Therefore, the integrity of data and events presented in the courtroom is directly related to this reality and should be adjudged with this evidence integrity risk in mind. In other words, the integrity of digital data, upon which facts in litigation are based, is not absolute as long as it is subject to threats and is vulnerable to alteration.

2.4. Finding a Role for the Digital Forensic Expert Witness

Unlike many of the traditional fields of forensics, such as firearms or latent fingerprint comparison, or forensic pathology and the medical determination of cause and manner of death, information technology and digital forensic expertise must often be shared incrementally in separate stages, beginning with the most basic concepts, repeatedly and in different styles, to the different players at the progressive stages of the litigation of a case. To begin with, assuming that the expert and the advocate are able to communicate and a professional relationship is formed to have the expert work on some digital forensic problem in a particular case, the sponsoring attorney may or may not have mastered some or all of the techniques that will be applied in a particular assignment and in any event will need to rely on the expert's expertise as events unfold in the course of pretrial litigation and in contending with opposing experts. Trial judges, who will preside over the pretrial stages as well as the jury trial, are also lawyers by training and experience, and the same calculations as to the technological sophistication (or lack thereof) of the court will need to be made and recalibrated by both the attorney and the expert as the litigation proceeds and challenges are mounted against the expert's own qualifications, methods or conclusions, or the expert is called upon to assist in the challenge of an opposing expert.

By and large, the most effective method of communicating complex information is the narrative, and therefore technical experts need to become "story tellers" if they wish to become more effective forensic witnesses. Testimony requires the narrative to take shape in the form of questions and answers, which may seem counterproductive to the telling of a good story, but with practice the routine of fitting the relevant information into a narrative format within the "Q and A" ritual of the courtroom can become second nature to an accomplished expert. The expert's story of his or her forensic investigation will usually tie together one or more of the following matters, as most digital forensic investigations will cover over similar ground.

2.4.1. Who?

The expert will often attempt to identify the suspected individuals who were responsible for the forensic artifacts or digital evidence found. This will entail determining who had access and whether there are network connections leading to others with potential access. The expert will attempt to determine who discovered the evidence and perhaps who should have but did not discover it. Those who may have initially investigated the incident or the suspicious acts reported and who obtained any original evidence or handled the evidence will also need to be identified and placed in context. As with any investigation, chronologies, often with multiple tracks, will need to be constructed to make sense of the different roles that different individuals played in causing, detecting, investigating, and analyzing the suspected acts and resulting evidence.

2.4.2. What?

There is some specific things that experts typically do with various forensic tools to identify, collect, preserve, and analyze the data that has been and is being considered. A report will need to be prepared identifying the various devices, network connections, software, and logging that is relevant. Reports, tests conducted, and notes will usually be required to be turned over to the opposing attorney and any opposing experts for their critique. Forensic practice differs in one important way from what the same expert might do to investigate and memorialize a confidential business audit of a particular computer or network. Because everything that is committed to an electronic, audio, or written record is likely to be disclosed in the course of litigation, attorneys who work with experts will encourage them not to record their thought processes or even their initial formulations of their conclusions because they will be used to develop lines of impeachment by the opposing attorney. Like the question-and-answer format for forensic story telling, this may at first seem awkward to the beginning expert. There are countless examples of experts who have been unnecessarily harassed by lines of questions based on their initial thoughts and jottings that have been turned into contradictions and doubts about their ultimate conclusions and opinions by skilled cross-examiners at *Daubert* hearings and trials.

2.4.3. Where?

Digital forensic experts need to have analogies, metaphors, and effective visual aides prepared to allow technophobic judges and jurors to follow the discussion of places that are constantly changing between actual physical locations and virtual places in digital media or in network spaces that are sources of digital evidence. Once again, like reports, the chain of custody will often need to make clear where in the digital environment evidence was located. When describing the physical locations of the various relevant actors, devices, and network connections, the expert should attempt to be as comprehensive as possible in determining the security precautions, including both systematic and ad hoc efforts to secure access to and from those locations and to any network connections that were or were not accurately monitored or recorded.

2.4.4. When?

Obviously, together with the preceding general categories that are covered by the forensic expert in the course of an investigation and recounted in reports and testimony, the expert will attempt to identify when relevant things happened and to conform the different time stamps and recording of events on different devices and in different time zones. Adjustments will often need to be made in erroneous time reporting due to improper or contradictory settings on various interconnected devices that are involved in the investigation. Like most other technical inconsistencies that can be adequately explained, the use of appropriate visual aides will be crucial to ensuring that the fact finders can follow the expert's reconstruction of the actual chronology and or apparent synchronicity of events.

2.4.5. How?

The key concept for effective expert testimony is the appearance and reality of objectivity. This means the objectivity and lack of bias of the expert and of the tool and technique selection and application to address the assignment. For example, in a battle of experts, the expert who has attempted to find and consider all of the relevant evidence that argues against his or her conclusions and to explain those contrary or contradictory matters will be seen as far more objective and as unbiased when compared with an expert who failed to consider the opposing evidence or who simply tries to argue that it is not worth considering, when in fact it is. Because the expert will be working with one side of a legal case, in an advocacy arena, either preparing the case or preparing the attorney to cross-examine the opposing expert, it is extremely difficult to avoid becoming, and thus being seen to be, a part of an advocacy team. This appearance needs to be avoided by the expert if his or her testimony is to be understood by the fact finder as independent of the obvious advocacy of not only the attorneys but also by opposing experts.

2.5. Finding the Right Style: Getting Beyond "Them That Can't"

In addition to mastering the tools and techniques that comprise the state of the art of the digital forensic expert, to be effective, the expert must be able to quickly bring the various role players in the world of litigation up to speed to be able to make use of his or her understanding and explanations of the issues under investigation. There is an old saying with variations on the theme "He who can, does. He who cannot teaches," attributed to George Bernard Shaw, or what has been called H. L. Mencken's Law: "Those who can—do. Those who can't—teach." One suspects that these men never met a teacher they did not dislike.

Many people, including most jurors, have one or two favorite teachers. Think about the skills that your favorite teachers had during your school days. To have left a lasting impression on you during your formative years, they probably included one or more of the following: they made learning complex or difficult new material fun; they had more than one costume or persona that they used to create an interest in very different types of students and groups; they knew when to digress from the lesson plan and to reveal some or all of the process that they themselves had used to understand the subject matter; they invited you to disagree with their working hypothesis without jeopardizing the authority inherent in the teacher–student relationship that had been nurtured; and, they occasionally succeeded in making you an advocate for or against one or more of the central ideas that were being taught.

Finally, you must be prepared to teach 12 jurors how to use your expertise or to abuse the mistaken conclusions of an opposing expert about complex questions of cause and effect concerning the relevant electronic evidence in a case. Although teaching may not be your chosen overall style, you will nevertheless need to develop the same sorts of skills and patience with the abilities of your various audiences that make professional educators remembered for being great teachers, if you are to succeed at all levels of performance as a technical expert witness.

3. THE PERFORMANCE

Whenever the expert appears to be operating off of a script, presumably prepared by the advocate, without regard for the constraints of widely recognized principles, theories, and methods that are appropriate for addressing a particular problem, he or she risks being seen as just another blockhead, perched on the lap of the lawyer, acting as ventriloquist. Such an interaction between the lawyer and the expert risks making the witness appear to be manipulated and unbelievable. Seeing through the expert's advocacy is a little like seeing the ventriloquist's lips moving. It is almost inevitable that to the extent this picture forms in the minds of the jurors, extreme bias and a total lack of credibility will be the most likely conclusions to be reached about the combined performance of the expert and attorney by the fact finders. But people do see the lips moving and they still love to watch a master ventriloquist perform.

Therefore, the performance of an objective expert witness being questioned by the sponsoring attorney should strive to make transparent the fact that he or she has been hired to do an important professional job. There is nothing wrong with acknowledging that the expert is being paid (and hopefully paid well!) for applying the expertise that has developed over a career or even a lifetime of carefully considering scientific and technical solutions to one or more of the relevant issues in the litigation. In the best forensic testimony, there is never any attempt to create the illusion of expertise available on the cheap, if only because it is so easily exposed by cross-examination. The fact that the expert's services are paid for is easily accepted by the jury, who may even attach more authority to a witness whose time is worth something and then they can more easily give their rapt attention to a carefully constructed narrative of how the expert proceeded to go to work, applying the recognized theories and methods of the relevant technical and scientific communities of interest.

It is always up to the cooperative effort of the trial lawyer and the testifying expert to overcome the concern that jurors instinctively feel about testimony that is offered for a price. This is true whether that testimony is offered for a fee by a Nobel Prize–winning scientist or a plea bargaining, convicted inmate who is "snitching" on his cellmate in exchange for a reduction in his sentence (see David Goldblat, *Art and Ventriloquism*, Routledge, New York, 2006).

In other words, in the course of the qualification of the expert and during the rendition of the testimony, a fact finder needs to understand why it is crucial for the forensic expert to have his or her own independent voice. The fact finder needs to be able to understand enough of the basis for the expert's opinions, without being able to understand everything the expert knows, to be able to rely on the expert's conclusion in deciding the case. To the extent that the expert has a track record of appearing for both plaintiffs and defendants, it helps to assure the fact finder that the expert is in demand for his or her knowledge and experience and is not just a niche specialist, marketing only to plaintiffs, prosecutors, or defendants as the case may be. Similarly, experts' reputations for a lack of bias and high personal and professional standards are enhanced to the extent that they become known for turning down requests for services, when in fact their expertise is not appropriate for the proposed assignment.

4. A SPRINT THROUGH THE HISTORY OF THE JURY TRIAL IN THE UNITED STATES

Before considering the particular requirements that attend IT technical testimony as a factual or an expert witness at trial, a brief history of the evolution of trial by jury, as it evolved first in Great Britain and then in the United States, will help to place in context the role of witnesses in general and shed light on the different rules that apply to the testimony of factual witnesses and to the special case of the expert. Although it is true that the paid witness is a striking exception to the rules, the use of them, as experts, has become pervasive.

Toward the end of the seventeenth century, shortly after the authorities became disabused of the general use of torture to extract confessions from witches who they wished to burn, as the powerful magistrate judges in the colonies slowly lost their decision-making control over serious criminal trials, and rules of evidence began to protect the accused, who began to be represented by counsel against charges brought by professional prosecutors, something that began to resemble the modern jury trial ritual came to be favored. This new ritual moved away from invoking divine inter-vention or complete reliance on extracting coerced confessions through the techniques developed by the Inquisition toward recognition of the need to produce witnesses with knowledge of relevant facts. Slowly the accused began to be allowed to testify and to present evidence in his or her behalf at the trial. The presentation of testimony by these witnesses was increasingly controlled by the lawyers who contributed to the devel-opment of a growing law of evidence to control the admission of evidence through factual testimony of witnesses with knowledge about the case. These witnesses with knowledge began to replace the swearing contests by prominent citizens for or against the victim or the accused, which had long been the custom, since trials by ordeals, such as throwing witches into bogs, as depicted in the witch scene in *Monty Python's Holy Grail*, had fallen out of favor.

That world and our individual and collective experience of it turns out to be a most ambiguous place, with or without the tools and techniques developed through the disciplines of science and technology. For centuries, plagues and epidemics of all kinds were thought to be caused by miasmas of the air, moving like odors in the wind, from person to person, and thereby spreading contagion, wherever the miasmas persisted and found new victims to infect. The most intelligent scholars and thinkers of all of the affected European societies throughout the Middle Ages steadfastly refused to question this fallacy and as a result were completely unable to affect the devastation of each succeeding epidemic. Regardless of the lack of success that their practical efforts had over time, they consistently rationalized those failures in ways that allowed them to maintain their foolish casual explanations.

Gradually, the scientific method began to be applied to military, engineering, business, and medical problems, like the problem of contagion. In 1854, Sir John Snow set out to refute the theory of miasmas, still in vogue, and began to investigate a particularly virulent cholera epidemic that had killed hundreds in central London. He created a famous map of the area of London where deaths attributed to cholera had taken place and was able to visualize the scatter pattern of all of these fatalities as they were added to his map. The map showed a definite center to the contagion, which by the process of elimination was proved to be a pump located on Broad Street, at the epicenter of the places where the victims had died.

Where areas within the scatter pattern showed no fatalities, Snow was able to prove that the people in those areas had another source of drinking water. In one apparent anomaly, the explanation turned out to be that the particular block where none had died during the epidemic was in fact a brewery, where everyone consumed beer, rather than the contaminated water from the Broad Street pump that was the source of the cholera epidemic. Snow followed up his visual proof with a lengthy report that set out all of the arguments that had been made in support of the miasma theory of the cholera contagion and showed with evidence that they failed to explain the observed and uncontradicted facts, relevant and material to the epidemic of 1854. After conclusively refuting the old theories, Snow showed that the contagion could only be reasonably explained by the new theory; namely, that the cholera was spread by a contaminated water source, consumed by each of the victims.

We live in another time, perhaps somewhat more enlightened, at least to the extent that we have learned to question even the most fashionable learned theories themselves, as well as the observed inefficacious methods of solving particular problems. This may be one of the reasons that today, in lieu of torturing the accused to obtain a confession, or subjecting them to some other ordeal to invoke divine intervention and thereby proceed to the execution, in serious litigation about complex issues, opposing experts are called to assist the jury in sorting out all of the available explanations for particular effects, or pieces of evidence, such as the presence of an e-mail on a particular computer hard drive but not on another; browser records of visits to terrorist or child pornography Web sites; fragments of deleted files that correlate to dates after the owner learned that he was suspected of a crime.

5. IT EXPERTS AND EXPLICIT CHALLENGES TO ELECTRONIC EVIDENCE

Courts in the United States generally presume that records created in the normal course of business are authentic and can be rebutted by any direct evidence to the contrary *(18)*. Absent specific evidence that tampering occurred, the mere possibility of tampering does not affect the authenticity of a computer record *(19)*. The fact that it is possible to alter computer data is plainly insufficient to establish untrustworthiness *(20)*. Further, any allegations of computer record alteration not accompanied by evidence of tampering goes to their weight, not admissibility *(21)*. Normally, however, courts will disallow challenges to the authenticity of computer-based evidence absent a specific showing that the computer data in question may not be accurate or genuine—mere speculation and unsupported theories generally will not suffice *(22)*.

This application of authenticity controls was illustrated at a district court evidentiary hearing where the defendant challenged the admission of chat logs, claiming that the government failed to lay a sufficient foundation. The defendant argued that the chat room printouts were incomplete and that undetectable "material alterations" of log content or names could have been made by the government. The district court allowed the logs and said that such claims went to the weight of the logs, not their admissibility *(23)*. Authenticity was demonstrated by testimony from the government expert explaining the creation of the logs with his computer. Further, he testified that the printouts appeared to be an accurate representation of the chat room conversations among the parties to the communications, even though the printouts did not contain deleted information. This testimony was adequate to allow a reasonable juror to find that the chat room log printouts were authenticated.

At issue in *People v. Lugashi (24)* was the authentication of computer-based evidence in a criminal prosecution for credit card fraud. This evidence was offered through the testimony of a systems administrator of the bank. The defense challenged this employee's ability to authenticate the computer-generated records, claiming that she was not a computer expert; she was not involved in the programming, design, and operation of the bank's internal systems; and her testimony was hearsay insofar as her understanding of the system's functioning came from other technical staff.

The court rejected this argument and ruled that "a person who generally understands the system's operation and possesses sufficient knowledge and skill to properly use the system and explain the resultant data, even if unable to perform every task from initial design and programming to final printout, is a 'qualified witness'" for purposes of establishing a foundation for the computer evidence *(25)*. The court also commented that the defendant's proposed requirement for computer expertise would require production of "hordes" of technical witnesses that would unduly burden both the already crowded trial courts and the business employing such technical witnesses "to no real benefit" *(26)*.

The issue in *US v. Wilson (27)* was whether the government's use of computer log evidence proved by a preponderance of evidence that an electronic document was sent. At an evidentiary hearing in July 2001, the government Office of Indian Affairs (OIA) introduced log records showing that a particular letter was sent in November 1993. This log evidence was introduced by an employee who testified that if an entry was made in this log, the entry signified that the document had been sent. The defendant countered that in the time between when the proof was requested and the actual hearing, OIA upgraded its document tracking system and converted it to a new Oracle program. The claim, thus, was that the system could have been tampered with or an entry could have been added just recently to reflect the past transmission. The court ruled that the government had not met its burden of proving the transmission of data via the log evidence. Specifically, the court based this on the questionable circumstances surrounding the government's production of the correspondence log; the inadequacy of the testifying witness' capacity to authenticate the logs (the witness neither worked in the OIA docketing unit nor was she personally responsible for drafting, typing, copying, or sending out the document in question); and, the government's failure to call another pertinent witness.

A very similar ruling was pronounced in a U.S. district court case concerning the reliability of IRS computer evidence *(28)*. The government presented a computer-generated printout supporting its assertion that a Notice of Demand had been sent on a particular date and time. The court rejected its assertion that this printout established an irrebuttable presumption that the notice was in fact sent *(29)*. Instead it found that the government's inability to reconcile the irregularities between when the IRS said the mailing of the computer-generated records occurred and when its computers are programmed to send the mailing rendered it unreliable to prove compliance with legal requirements. The court queried, "[H]ow can this inconsistency be explained without resulting in uncertainty as to the accuracy of [the dates in question]" *(30)*?

For parties seeking to exclude digital evidence, these cases support a strategy that hones in on inconsistencies in the digital evidence collection and storage, both on the technical and human fronts. While increasing automation will diminish the number of witnesses qualified to authenticate computer-generated evidence like logs, inconsistencies at the human–computer interface—the collecting, processing, and storing of logs as evidence of electronic events—may provide fodder for digital evidence opponents to rebut the current relatively low threshold of proving authenticity and reliability and force proponents of digital evidence to offer more comprehensive foundational proof *(31)*.

6. IT EXPERTS AS A SOLUTION TO THE AMBIGUOUS TREATMENT OF ELECTRONIC EVIDENCE

Challenges to computer log evidence reliability can take the form of questioning the authenticity of digital records by suggesting that digital evidence is not original or has been altered, showing that the technology producing the logs is unreliable, or failing to connect the evidence with its source (i.e., proving identity) *(32)*. Specifically, an opponent of the logs may argue:

1. Electronic evidence bias, in other words, that digital logs are incomplete or incomprehensive for the time frame surrounding the event in question, or that the technology responsible for the logs (computer hardware and/or software) failed to capture of all relevant events (network traffic, etc.).
2. Electronic evidence does not prove identity.
3. Electronic evidence may have been altered prior to, during, or after collection.
4. Electronic evidence is not "original," which is to say it has been processed from its primary form (zeros and ones in machine code) into a human-readable format usable by analysis and presentation tools.
5. Electronic evidence is hearsay and does not satisfy the business records exception *(33)*.

Absent an opponent proving beyond a mere "possibility" that digital evidence is untrustworthy, electronic evidence will ordinarily be admitted under current precedent via a foundational showing that the testifying witness had firsthand knowledge of the evidence; by taking judicial notice of its authenticity as the product of an automated process or system; or that the digital record(s) are shown to meet the business records exception to the Hearsay Rule. In all of these scenarios, the authenticity control utilized by courts is a witness who can testify as to the proper functioning of the equipment producing the electronic evidence. In other words, courts interpret compliance with legal reliability standards by measuring the narration, perception, and memory of a witness, subject to judicial controls such as the oath, the personal presence of the witness in relation to the evidence to be given, subjection to cross-examination, and/or qualifications as a technical expert. Legal standards have been interpreted and applied in deference to judicial efficiency and business practice; the Federal Rules of Evidence (FREs) are no exception. For example, the Business Records Exception to the Hearsay Rule allows records containing out-of-court statements into evidence because of the necessity and reliance by business, and consequently, is therefore probative in resolving disputes. The trust guarantee is that businesses need to keep accurate records in order to conduct business, and "if business relies on it, why shouldn't the courts" *(34)*? So, for instance, if the ledger records are kept in the course of regularly conducted business activity, recorded on/about the time of occurrence, and it is the regular practice of business to make such records, a human connected to those processes can authenticate them for admissibility purposes. In the digital realm, the author is the computer (in whole or in part), so courts authenticate by requiring evidence (process or system producing computer data) to be accurate and reliable.

Whether the log is treated akin to a paper document or photograph (in which case the standard is self-authentication), reliability is inferred from presuming that what the testifying witness observes is real, that deliberate alterations are rare, and that mistakes are obvious *(35)*. However, digital evidence is distinguishable in that alterations are not obvious; there is a low barrier to entry for alteration; and the human operator's perception is based on what the computer told him or her as opposed to having a witness inside the machine. The problem with extending traditional reliability controls to digital evidence is that the "event collection and storage" evidenced by logs are a function of the computer's memory, perception, and bias, yet courts are controlling against fraud by measuring human interaction with the computers producing the log evidence (indirect controls).

7. THE CRIME SCENE INVESTIGATION© (CSI) PHENOMENON AND ITS IMPACT ON DIGITAL FORENSICS

Many members of the consuming public, whether technophile or technophobe, have developed great expectations about the power of forensic science based on the repeated successes of their favorite fantasy forensic scientists. They may believe these actors and actresses are performing based on real scientific methods and can unerringly solve the most complex evidentiary problems, as projected in countless crime-solving episodes on television. These expectations are constantly being heightened by new iterations of the same themes, produced by the extremely popular CSI entertainment industry. Among other citizens selected to decide civil and criminal cases are the fans of these programs.

Whether or not jurors for a particular case loyally program their TiVo's so as not to miss a single forensic melodrama, we can deduce from Nielsen's ratings that society has embraced the 2-minute sound-bite caricatures of forensics as reality. The effect is to paint oftentimes unrealistic expectations about the abilities of forensic scientists. These unrealistic expectations of forensic experts' qualifications and capabilities are often in turn juxtaposed with the imagined possibilities engendered by the obvious advances in technology. This conceptual convergence of technology as a manifestation of imaginations that is reflected in the operational reality of forensic practitioners has blurred the line between what might be "possible" versus what a juror may believe was "probably possible." The challenge for forensic experts is to avoid falling down the slippery slope into science-fiction land and to present findings and opinions grounded in legal proof that are simultaneously informed by realistic assessments of the art and science of forensics taken together with actual capabilities of available advances in technology. The CSI phenomenon can make the job of actually being an objective forensic expert witness extremely challenging, and an expert needs to be aware of its existence when preparing to explain both the power and the limits of digital forensic methods. Beyond getting the theories, methods, and conclusions right and testifying about the actual results of a forensic assignment in court, the forensic scientist must also be able to clearly explain the difference between the arts of the CSI entertainer and the methods of and limitations on the practicing digital forensic scientist or technical expert.

7.1. IT Experts as Reliability Controls: What Is the Lynchpin of Credibility?

Is the lynchpin of credibility for electronic data derived from the technology (computer hardware and software) or from the person who collects, synthesizes, and interprets the electronic data and events *(36)*? In other words, answering "who is the real witness" should dictate how courts should measure the trustworthiness of "statements" made in logs or other digital evidence *(37)*. The nature of log evidence, unlike instances where a human is putting a pen or typewriter to paper, suggests that the "real witness" is the chain of digital events surrounding the creation, transportation, and storage of logs. IT experts should be poised to serve as the "eyewitness in the machine" and narrow the abstractions between how digital activities are re-created to portray the truth in litigation.

7.2. Digital Data Reliability Amidst Threats and Vulnerabilities

No matter "how" courts measure trustworthiness of digital evidence [cf. Federal Rules of Evidence 901(b)*(9)*; 901(a); or 803*(6)*], it is important to note that there is a trump clause underlying each rule that can turn this presumption of admissibility on its head. Namely, "…if the source, method, or circumstance of preparation indicate lack of trustworthiness *(38)*." As digital evidence is increasingly used to resolve legal disputes, focus will shift from presumptively ushering in the digital traces of business activities to disputing the digital evidence used to buttress legal claims. Attempts to discredit digital evidence will accompany this shift, and the technical experts who understand the mutable attributes of electronic data will be tapped for their knowledge that alterations (insertions, deletions, modifications) are not only possible but also probable and oftentimes incapable of being detected. This will be exacerbated by the emergence of software programs that expand data alteration capabilities to anyone with point-and-click capabilities, where it is not necessary to have technical knowledge and skills to manually weave through electronic data and manipulate certain bits to reflect factual changes. For example, automated data-wiping techniques/software *(39)* is prevalent and easily accessible. It is only a matter of time before software that performs more surgical alteration becomes mainstream such that instead of wholesale deletion/removal of data, it will be trivial to change "John Doe" to "Jane Doe" or host computer "198.254.14.128" *(40)* (corresponding with John's workstation) to be "198.254.14.122" (corresponding with Jane's workstation).

The evidentiary significance is that continued reliance upon controls such as "proper functioning of the computer producing the digital evidence" do not adequately address the already existing threats to evidentiary integrity.

8. DAUBERT: EXPANDING STANDARDS OF JUDICIALLY DETERMINED ADMISSIBILITY

As citizens and potential jurors have come to expect definitive answers as to cause and effect from expert witnesses who are called by one of the parties to testify in a trial, the U.S. Supreme Court, in a series of decisions beginning with *Daubert v. Merrell Dow Pharmaceuticals, Inc.*, 509 U.S. 579 (1993), has imposed a gatekeeping role for judges. Frustrated with the number of cases that had highlighted the lack of reliability of a great deal of the expert testimony that was being permitted by trial judges, pursuant to the rules of evidence, the Court held that it was the job of the trial judge to screen the admissibility of expert witness testimony before allowing a given expert to take the stand and give an opinion about some issue that was in contention in the case.

Prior to *Daubert*, existing case law had generally upheld the discretion of the trial judge in admitting all expert testimony, where the expert testified that he was qualified as an expert and that his methods were generally recognized by his peers within his area of expertise. In applying Federal Rule of Evidence 702, the Court decided to set out a number of flexible standards to guide courts in ruling on the admissibility of a given expert's opinion. Since the *Daubert* decision, FRE 702 has been amended to track more closely the Court's ruling and the standards for determining reliability. It is now the basic expert witness rule in all federal courts and in the majority of states. The rule makes an exception to the general rule that witnesses may only testify about facts and with narrow exceptions are generally forbidden from giving their opinions about the evidence. Today, the rule reads as follows:

> Rule 702. Testimony by Expert: scientific, technical, or other specialized knowledge will assist the trier of fact to understand the evidence or to determine a fact in issue, a witness qualified as an expert by knowledge, skill, experience, training, or education, may testify thereto in the form of an opinion or otherwise, if *(1)* the testimony is based upon sufficient facts or data, *(2)* the testimony is the product of reliable principles and methods, and *(3)* the witness has applied the principles and methods reliably to the facts of the case.

In applying the gatekeeping standards established for scientific expert witness testimony in the *Daubert* decision, and extended to cover technical expertise in *Kumho Tire Co., Ltd. v. Carmichael,* 526 U.S. 137 (1999), courts have stepped up their scrutiny of the qualifications of technical experts and of the reliability of their theories, methods, and results. What began as a fairly simple template to test the qualifications and the reliability of the methods and conclusions testified about by forensic expert witnesses has mushroomed into a kind of trial within the trial, where experts of all kinds are challenged, based on the expanding case law that has attempted to apply the standards first announced by the Supreme Court in the *Daubert* and *Kumho Tire* cases. Initially, the Court suggested that when an expert or his opinion was challenged before trial that an initial judicial review of the proffered expert testimony should include an inquiry into whether the theory used was testable or falsifiable and whether it had been adequately tested. Any known error rate attributed to the methods employed should be considered. Evidence of general agreement through peer review by the relevant expert community as to the relevance of the theories and the reliability of the methods should be considered. Finally, the fit of the theory, methods, and conclusions to the significant issues in the case should be determined by the court and satisfy the court that the opinions offered by the expert were helpful to the jury in sorting out a relevant complex issue, without intentionally or inadvertently invading the province of the fact finders.

Since *Daubert*, and through its progeny, these fairly simple and intuitive standards for the admissibility of forensic expert testimony have expanded as Charles Dickens predicted in *Bleak House*. "The one great principle of the English Law is to make business for itself. There is no other principle distinctly, certainly and consistently maintained through all its narrow turnings. Viewed by this light, it becomes a coherent scheme, and not the monstrous maze the laity are apt to think it." Without citing the thousands of cases that have been decided concerning whether or not the trial judges have succeeded in properly admitting or excluding expert testimony, the list of standards found to be relevant for consideration has expanded from four or five to dozens. These standards now include many additional considerations. To name but a few:

1. Requiring precise explanations of each step in the expert's reasoning, methodology, or the application of the various principles leading up to each and every conclusion; presenting all sources for each factual base and any and all assumptions used by the expert.
2. Describing other facts and/or assumptions that were available to the expert but which were not used and the reasons why they were excluded from consideration.
3. Providing, in addition to the testability of any method or process of reasoning and the results of all such tests, information about whether the tests reported could be or were repeated by the expert and whether there were any other test protocols that could or should have been used to test the expert's methods or hypothesis.
4. Including just what professional standards apply to the work in this case and how they apply and whether there was any departure from those standards in the work done in this case.

Robert Whitney has examined this expansion in his article, "A Practicing Guide to the Application of *Daubert* and *Kumho*," published in the *American Journal of Trial Advocacy* (Vol. 23, p. 241, 1999).

It is perhaps helpful to return to the original impetus of the move away from attorney carte blanche in the selection of experts and whatever opinions they cared to offer and to conceive of the *Daubert* gatekeeping standards as a template for judges to check against the qualifications and work that the challenged expert has to offer. More experienced and sophisticated jurists may have a long list of related questions to put to the expert in the event that opposing counsel fails to raise all of the relevant issues. Such a judge has learned over countless cases the few really important things that are essential to consider before reaching a decision as to whether the expert being examined is truly trying to help resolve a significant complex issue. For more experienced attorneys and judges, a hearing may not be required to determine that a proffered expert is simply making up stuff to either confuse the jury or to advocate a position that is insufficiently supported by the state of knowledge or scientific methods known to be reliable in relation to solving similar problems.

To succeed in testifying at trial as an expert requires the witness to develop the attitude of initially questioning the sponsoring attorney about the significance of the issues to be investigated and analyzed until the expert is completely clear that his or her expertise is appropriate for the assignment. If the assignment is accepted, the work that is undertaken must be accompanied by consistent criticism of all theories, approaches, methods, and testing that are used in the process of reaching a conclusion or opinion about the issues considered. A forensic expert must assume that each conclusion that is published and testified about will be tested by cross-examination and opposing expert testimony. Only by consistently considering all other reasonable explanations for the observations and conclusions can the expert be adequately prepared for what comes at trial or before if the expert is challenged as to either his qualifications or his methods and conclusions.

When the courts decided to set out a simplistic philosophy of science, together with the traditional reliance on well-known institutional certification of individual experts (which formed the basis of the new standards of reliability for all expert testimony), there was no mention in the early cases of the evidence created by computers as being any sort of a special case. Both the sciences, such as physics and chemistry, and the technical skill fields, such as engineering and latent fingerprint comparison, had long traditions and in most cases university or institutionalized training programs with forms of certification or licensing to recognize experts in good standing within their socially recognized areas of scientific or technical expertise. So, it behooves the digital forensic expert to plan ahead for bridging the conceptual gaps that loom between what judges and juries have come to expect by way of qualifications of more traditional experts and what is required for competent IT experts to claim entitlement to the same exceptional treatment under the rules of evidence and the case law that applies to all expert witnesses.

8.1. Satisfying the Gatekeeper

Since the *Daubert* decision, the kinds of challenges that have been mounted against both suspect pseudosciences and previously unassailable, traditional fields of forensic expertise have contributed to an entire literature in the legal and professional journals. For a sampling of this literature and analysis of the decisions on a jurisdictional basis that directs the reader to courts in geographic areas of particular interest, see http://www.daubertontheweb.com/. As might be expected, different results have been obtained from different courts (theoretically applying the same standards to similar experts and their opinions), and decisions need to be analyzed on the basis of the often case-specific facts and the subtle differences in qualifications and experience between opposing experts. This wide range of rulings is perhaps most effectively revealed by comparing two opinions by the same judge in a case that featured an assault on the traditionally accepted reliability of fingerprint comparison expert witness testimony, announced in *United States of America v. Carlos Ivan Llera Plaza, Acosta, and Rodriquez*, 179 F. Supp.2d 492 (decided Jan. 7, 2002, E. Dist. PA).

After the first *Daubert* challenge hearing, the trial judge found that the evidence introduced by the government to support the scientific *bona fides* of the discipline of fingerprint comparison did not square with the requirements of *Daubert*. The court found that the method used by the FBI fingerprint expert (referred to as the ACE-V, or analysis, comparison, evaluation, and verification method) did not adequately satisfy a number of the gatekeeping standards established by *Daubert* and applied to technical disciplines such as fingerprint comparison by *Kumho Tire*. These shortcomings included failing to persuade the court as to the scientific criterion of testing or peer review, the criterion for determining the rate of error, and the operation of the applied method under uniformly accepted scientific standards.

And so, to the delight of the defense and the disbelief of the prosecution, Federal District Judge J. Pollak, granted the defense motion challenging the admissibility of an experienced FBI fingerprint expert and decided that he could not testify that the defendant's prints matched prints found at the scene because the government had failed to prove that the ACE-V method operated under uniformly accepted "scientific" standards and therefore failed under the *Daubert* and *Kumho Tire* tests. Needless to say, after nearly a century of having expert fingerprint opinions as to the certainty of a match between a print found on evidence at a crime scene and a print obtained from the defendant being routinely accepted by almost every court in the land in criminal prosecutions, this decision caused a furor in the law enforcement community and sent academics scurrying to publish a new barrage of articles on the wisdom or folly of allowing courts to exclude opinions from forensic experts from trial.

The government quickly requested a rehearing of the court's initial opinion excluding the testimony of the fingerprint expert. At the second, lengthy evidentiary hearing, additional experts from the United States and abroad were called by the government to testify about the factors that the court had initially found lacking after the initial hearing. Of particular interest to digital forensic experts, the court found that lacking specific tests in the *Daubert* sense that provide reasonable measures of the reliability of the proffered expert testimony, the question for a *Daubert* challenge court is whether, in the absence of such tests, a court should conclude that the system under consideration, as practiced by recognized experts, "has too great a likelihood of producing erroneous results to be admissible as evidence in a courtroom setting." In deciding to admit the opinions of the experienced FBI fingerprint examiner in this case, the court held:

> ...I have found, on the record before me that there is no evidence that certified FBI fingerprint examiners present erroneous identification testimony, and, as a corollary, that there is no evidence that the rate of error of certified FBI fingerprint examiners is unacceptably high.

Both of the opinions should be carefully studied to comprehend the thinking of one well-respected jurist struggling to apply the gatekeeping standards and to consider what evidence is more or less persuasive to a judge in the final analysis. [For the second opinion, see *United States of America v. Carlos Ivan Llera Plaza, Acosta, and Rodriquez* , 188 F. Supp.2d 549 (decided March 13, 2002, E. Dist. PA)]. In addition to being available online, a more comprehensive discussion of these opinions (including the full text of the March reconsideration) and their impact on information technology expert witness testimony is available in *A Guide To Forensic Testimony: The Art and Practice of Presenting Testimony as an Expert Technical Witness* (Fred Chris Smith and Rebecca Gurley Bace, Addison-Wesley, Boston, 2003).

8.2. Life After Daubert: The Technical Expert's Role at Trial

In *State v. Guthrie* (627 N.W. 2d 401, 2001 S.D. 61, 2001), William Boyd Guthrie, a pastor in South Dakota, was convicted of the murder of his wife. The defendant claimed to have discovered the drug-laced, naked body of his dying wife in the bathtub of their home after returning from church. The defendant had recently obtained a large number of different sedatives, consistent with the drugs found in his deceased wife's body during autopsy. Prior to her death, there had been a number of close calls with household accidents involving electrical appliances falling into the wife's bath and her falling down the stairs (which appeared to have been tampered with) but that had not harmed the decedent. The prosecution presented evidence, including testimony by a computer forensics expert, that on the church computer, he found information that indicated that the defendant had recently searched the Web on sites that contained information about certain sedative pharmaceuticals, the fatal effects of drug overdoses, and various modes of accidental death.

After the state rested, defense counsel unveiled a "suicide note." Guthrie had given it to his attorney in mid-June, some 7 months earlier. Despite a reciprocal discovery order, counsel did not disclose the note because, as he explained to the judge the next day, it had been given to him "in confidence and [he] was not authorized to release it until yesterday." At the time he received it, counsel believed the document "could be as inculpatory as it was exculpatory, absent some authentication to its source. And particularly the elimination of my client as the source of the document." It did not occur to counsel to have the note examined for fingerprints until he read a newspaper article in the *Madison Daily Leader* in late December 1999 about Cynthia Orton's locally operated fingerprint business. Over the state's objection, the note was admitted, subject to state experts having an opportunity to examine it and a hearing following the trial on possible sanctions against defense counsel.

The unsigned note was dated the day before Sharon's death. It was addressed to her daughter:

> May 13,1999
> Dear Suzanne,
> I am sorry I ruined your wedding, Your dad told me about your concerns of my interfering in Jenalu's and the possibility I might ruin hers. I won't be there so put your mind at ease. You will understand after the wedding is done. I love you all Mom.

To prove the note was not written by Guthrie, the defense called a computer specialist who testified that in his examination of the contents of the church computer's hard drive, there were no traces of any such note ever having been created. However, prosecutors were reminded that there was a second computer. It had been in the Guthrie home. When officers had earlier examined the home in July with a search warrant, they saw the computer, but it appeared not to have been used. They decided not to take it. Guthrie had access to it until he was arrested and jailed on August 27. Sometime after his arrest, he asked his daughter and son-in-law, Suzanne and Les Hewitt, to store some of his household belongings, including this computer and the printer to which it was connected. Now on the revelation of a suicide note, the state asked Les Hewitt to bring in the computer. He agreed. Guthrie moved to suppress the evidence gained from this computer, asserting that it was seized illegally. The court denied the motion.

From examining the home computer's hard drive, the state's expert found a document with conspicuous similarities to the note Guthrie gave to his attorney. This document had been created and modified on August 7, 1999. Like the document portrayed to the jury as Sharon's "suicide note," it was dated May 13. The font appeared similar, and the margin size and spacing between words appeared identical, even the lack of a space in the date between the comma and 1999.

But there were also differences. The body of the note was missing; only the date and the words "I love you Mom" remained, but without the word "all" in that line. Nonetheless, based on his examination of the document's electronic background data and the similarities between the note Guthrie gave to his attorney and the document found on the home computer, the state's expert concluded that the August 7 document was the "predecessor" of the purported suicide note. According to the expert, additional lines could have been added, printed out, and the computer then turned off, and no record on the hard disk would remain of the added lines.

When recalled to the witness stand to answer whether he created the August 7 document, Guthrie testified, "I probably did, but I don't remember it." Even so, he insisted that he did not create the "suicide note" he found on June 10. To confirm that the note existed before August 7, attorney David Gienapp from defense counsel's law firm testified that he saw the note "quite a while before" July 26, 1999.

Still another note threatening suicide was found on the home computer's hard drive with Sharon again as the purported author. It listed various grievances Sharon addressed to Guthrie. One line stated, "I'm upset that you have had an affair and have not come clean with me, I have thought of ending my life and you would have to face up to it. Believe me I know how to do it." According to the state's expert, this document was created on August 11. Guthrie admitted he wrote this one, but merely as his way of working through the emotional trauma of Sharon's death, "to try to bring some reason into what had happened."

The Guthrie decision is of special interest to digital forensic experts for two reasons. First of all, it shows how during trial, new evidence or different interpretations of the evidence already admitted by the party for whom the expert is working may require additional forensic work on very short notice. Second, experts need to be very careful when faced with new midtrial assignments to be sure that their qualifications, including their training and experience with the particular technologies or tools that are the subject of the additional assignment, are within their expertise.

Here, assuming that the jury would conclude that the defendant and not his wife had used the church computer to browse the Web and to visit several incriminating sites, there was admissible evidence of the defendant's guilty intent, based on his search for ways to kill his wife and to make it look like either an accident or suicide. Because the prosecution had not seized all of the computers available to the defendant until the late arrival of the suicide note, the state elected to hire a "suicidologist" expert witness to testify that in his opinion the victim did not commit suicide. On appeal, the South Dakota Supreme Court found that it was error to allow a psychologist to give an expert opinion as to whether or not the victim had committed suicide, based on the total lack of any scientific basis to enable any expert to make such particular claims of expertise to enable him in turn to form an expert opinion about the state of mind of a particular victim.

Beyond the failure to comply with the *Daubert* gatekeeping standards, such expert opinions also risk being found on appeal to have invaded the province of the jury as to the ultimate issue in the case. In other words, with all of the available computer evidence, demonstrating both planning to make the murder look either like an accident or an intentional self-administered drug overdose and therefore a suicide, and the faking of a suicide note dated the day before the death on a separate computer, the government had solid, digital forensic evidence to present, without needing to risk a conviction on some other form of questionable expertise.

Guthrie is a good example of an increasing number of cases where the key to solving a question, traditionally addressed by other kinds of experts, such as whether the cause of death was murder, accident, or suicide, is in fact best addressed by a computer expert who has legitimately discovered and analyzed digital evidence that can be related to some issue in the case. *Guthrie* demonstrates that the best evidence of both the intent to kill the victim and then to try and cover it up, by making it look either accidental or suicidal, was in fact irrefutable, positive, digital evidence. Digital forensic experts may be of the greatest service in convincing trial lawyers of the availability and the power of digital evidence when involved in discussing trial strategies that involve computer evidence. Here the prosecutor would have been much better off with more computer evidence of guilt than attempting to counter the anticipated defense by calling a forensic psychologist, when the pathologist's autopsy was inconclusive or unpersuasive, to elicit an expert opinion based on the study of suicide, to in effect have that substitute expert render a conclusive opinion as to cause of death.

Although the conviction was ultimately upheld due to the weight of the other admissible evidence in the *Guthrie* case, rendering the error in admitting the suicidologist's opinion harmless, the lengthy discussion of the gatekeeper problems with the admission of the expert testimony echo the same concerns expressed by the judge in *United States of America v. Carlos Ivan Llera Plaza, Acosta, and Rodriquez*, discussed previously. It is one thing for an expert to point out that based on his experience and training, known suicides have a certain profile and known victims of accident or murder lack certain characteristics found in the suicide profile, and then leave it up to the jury to give such observations whatever weight they decide they are worth. It is quite another thing (and in the discipline of suicidology, the appellate court found that pursuant to the *Daubert* gatekeeping standards, there was simply no adequate scientific basis) to be allowed to render the opinion that a particular victim did or did not commit suicide. Digital forensic experts may face similar problems when asked to render opinions about who may or may not have created a particular piece of digital evidence that would require them to extend their claims of expertise beyond the reach of the gatekeeping standards.

8.3. Having the Best Résumé and a Better Method Can Make All the Difference

At the time that *Gates Rubber Company v. Bando Chemical Industries, Ltd., et al.*(167 F.R.D. 90, 1996, U.S. Dist. *LEXIS* 12423, decided May 1, 1996) was decided, it may have been the most heavily litigated case in Colorado. It certainly was the most heavily litigated digital forensic issue in the history of that state at that time. The plaintiff alleged that a former employee stole a valuable computer program when he left his employment and then attempted to delete word-processing files that contained evidence he had used the program at his new place of employment with Bando. The issue was whether the employee had intentionally destroyed evidence of the pending lawsuit or had acted reasonably by deleting files from his own hard disk after learning of the allegations against him and Bando, and then downloading the program and turning it over to his attorney. Both sides hired experts to assist the judge in determining what the actual facts were, and at the end of countless motions and hearings the judge made two rulings that point the way toward understanding what courts are looking for to help them decide when there is a battle of experts over a contested digital forensic issue.

The judge found that one expert was more qualified, and therefore more reliable than the other, holding:

> Bando's expert on matters associated with computer science was Robert Wedig, who holds a Ph.D. in computer science from Stanford. Wedig's credentials, experience and knowledge were impressive, and I relied upon his opinions. Gates failed to obtain a similar expert in timely fashion. Gates did offer the testimony of Robert Voorhees, the technician who was hired by Gates to copy the hard drive of the computer at Bando's Denver facility. His credentials, experience and knowledge were nowhere near those of Dr. Wedig, and I placed much less weight on his testimony than on Wedig's.

This is a reminder that the résumé is an extremely important document in any case where either the qualifications of an expert witness are challenged by the opposing attorney, with or without the assistance of an opposing expert, in a *Daubert* challenge hearing before trial, or where the judge is forced to choose between the experts as the fact finder. That résumé may very well be the first impression that the trial judge has of one's overall qualifications.

In this civil case, the trial judge was the fact finder of the underlying complex litigation and some rather serious sanctions hearings that arose because of the allegation that files and evidence had been destroyed. As to the sanctions litigation, after all was said and done, the court rendered a lengthy opinion that has been repeatedly used by other courts as precedent for the recognition of the forensic standard of making mirror images rather than merely copying hard drives with programs that alter and may delete some of the data:

> Gates argued that Voorhees did an adequate job of copying the Denver computer. Wedig persuaded me, however, that Voorhees lost, or failed to capture, important information because of an inadequate effort. In using Norton's Unerase, Voorhees unnecessarily copied this program onto the Denver computer first, and thereby overwrote 7 to 8 percent of the hard drive before commencing his efforts to copy the contents.
>
> Wedig noted that information which is introduced into a computer is distributed, in a random manner, to space which is not being used, or to space which contains a deleted file and is therefore available for use. To use Norton's Unerase, it was unnecessary for Voorhees to copy it onto the hard drive of the Denver computer. By doing so, however, the program obliterated, at random, 7 to 8 percent of the information which would otherwise have been available. No one can ever know what items were overwritten by the Unerase program.

Beyond the obvious value as legal precedent, mirroring the evolving standards for tools and techniques in the field of digital forensics, this opinion should be studied in its entirety to learn how one jurist weighed and then pieced together the competing opinions of the two IT expert witnesses, with complex factual claims by both sides, in order to reconstruct what happened to his satisfaction and to render a verdict. In this case, the defendant's forensic expert's opinion made all the difference and enabled the attorneys for the defendant to overcome some difficult facts with a better total explanation of what made the most sense, based on better theories, tools, techniques, and methods that were utilized by their IT expert.

9. THE CHALLENGE FOR IT EXPERTS: CAN HUMANS RELIABLY ADDRESS THE INTEGRITY OF ELECTRONIC DATA AND EVENTS?

Humans cannot offer direct eyewitness testimony of computer data processing in the same way they can make firsthand observations about an auto accident or the discharge of a weapon. People make inferences and draw conclusions using tools that indicate what is going on inside the computer and networks. Perhaps a system operator can testify that a program ran at a certain time on a certain computer based on a log indicating no error messages. However, the log is making a "statement" (i.e., a computer with IP address "xxx.yyy.zzz.1234" attempted to connect to port 80; or "littlejoe" user accessed the human resources directory on "3/3/01 at 0150 hours") based on its underlying programming. That log entry, however, could have been altered without any external indication; the data that the log is reporting on could have been altered without a log entry; or, the program that produced the logs could have been changed or run without a log entry.

The point is that any of these events could have happened without the operator's suspicion, yet his testimony about the proper functioning of the computer from which the logs were gathered would be the same. However, the efficient administration of justice, like many things in life, dictates that we place trust in facts not susceptible to observation. Realizing the threats and vulnerabilities attendant to the digital evidence that we rely upon to establish the truth of digital events, in conjunction with what is at stake in a dispute where digital evidence can be the sole source of proving/disproving a claim, IT expert testimony becomes crucial. And, to the extent that human fact-witness testimony is determined to be insufficient, second-order indications of digital evidence reliability, IT experts will increasingly be utilized as oracles for digital events *(41)*.

The evidentiary implications of the difference between digital and physical evidence challenge the presumption that humans are the optimal measures of digital evidence trustworthiness. For example, take the situation of a digital record that exists only as an aggregate of data pieces, knowing that distributed computing allows for data to be dispersed among desktops, network servers, laptops, back-up tapes, CD-ROMs, employee home computers, and PDAs. Humans are not present at every step of the data packet's path throughout the computing stream infrastructure, yet claim proof requires that triers of fact place trust in the re-creation of digital events, similar to how they rely on testimony by pathologists, chemists, and trace evidence analysts who reconstruct a physical homicide event.

Is ensuring the preseizure integrity of digital evidence of heightened significance compared with corporeal crime scenes? In other words, is there not the same risk that evidence may have been planted, altered, or wholesale removed prior to investigation—similar to moving or removing a gun, body, blood, physical document, and so forth? From a temporal perspective, it requires orders of magnitude less time to create and destroy digital evidence and its traces than it does for physical evidence. Also, traces of digital evidence and the tools to create/delete it are harder to identify, thus making it easier to fabricate/manipulate without detection.

For instance, one can remove a weapon or body and leave behind hair, fiber, or DNA unbeknownst and despite best efforts to cleanse the scene, whereas traces of digital information creation, manipulation, or destruction may not exist if system logging is not turned on. If logs are produced, oftentimes a miscreant has greater assurance of obfuscating the real illegal act because the location of all the inculpatory evidence is known by the criminal to reside in the logs. These attributes of digital crime scenes converge to enhance the likelihood of false-positive scenarios, making it much easier to fabricate a crime scene where there was no actual crime. Given that our justice system is appropriately weighted in favor of the accused (presumption of innocence unless proven guilty), opponents of inculpatory digital evidence and proponents of electronic equivalents of the "Chewbacca defense" *(42)* may find it easier to raise this challenge and cast doubt on the reliability of the proof being used against them.

The good news for technical experts may be that commercial software is increasingly being designed to conduct analysis tasks and automate domain knowledge and expertise. For instance, network intrusion tools are programmed to capture data that indicates an attack on a system, the conclusion being drawn from the algorithms that are coded into the program based on the expertise of its human developers. This "click button expertise" poses a challenge to legal rules governing the reliability of an expert's methodology and the underlying data *(43)*. It may also lead an opponent to query "Is the expert or the software performing the actual analysis?" If methodology is to be assessed, the analysis and methodology must be reproducible and transparent.

One state appellate court found that a computer forensic examiner's testimony about the results of analysis done by a computer program was not considered hearsay *(44)*. Even though the court recognized that information observed on the computer screen is arguably a "statement" by the computer and merely regurgitated by the expert, it nonetheless interpreted the analysis as computer-generated evidence that does not have to satisfy trust controls applied to hearsay evidence.

Given the number of programs that are involved in the creation, processing, and storage of information, the layers of abstraction and computer-generated hearsay applied to data may be numerous, and the number of appellate rulings to sort out just how many layers of traditional hearsay can be ignored or tolerated is speculative at best. The need for competent IT expert testimony that is clearly not hearsay is motivated by the need to facilitate a just legal framework for establishing the trustworthiness of digital evidence and to recognize the fundamental uncertainties in the processes involved in relying upon digital evidence to paint the facts that decide ultimate issues in litigation. These uncertainties risk being perpetuated if the assumptions underlying legal interpretations of the standards are institutionalized without proper measurement. This is the role that IT experts are going to be increasingly called upon to play in twenty-first century courtrooms.

REFERENCES AND NOTES

[1]For purposes of this chapter, the terms *electronic* and *digital* are used interchangeably. Similarly, *IT expert witness* refers to experts skilled in some aspect of information technology, including computer/digital forensics, which is the application of computer science principles, techniques, and methods to the identification, collection, preservation, analysis, and presentation of evidence.

[2]Examples of common logs that can be collected for audit purposes include, but are not limited to, the following: *Netflow logs* (records of unidirectional communications between computer ports across an instrumentation point on a network; data can include IP source/destination address pairs, packets per second, time stamps, byte count), *syslogs* (industry standard for capturing data about networked devices; data can include critical system events like reboots, login attempts, new account creation, termination of a particular host logging messages, etc.), *firewall logs* (computers that interface between the Internet and an internal network to implement a rule set

derived from an organization's access control policy), *IDS logs* (intrusion detection systems contain alerts that may indicate specific attacks on a host or network), *ARP cache* (tables containing data mapping IP addresses to physical hardware addresses, thus allowing computers to communicate with one another, useful for identifying IP addresses and devices connected to a network and determining connection activity of devices), *DNS cache* (tables that map IP addresses to hostnames), *routing table logs* (provide information on dropped or misrouted packets, false routing information, or disruption from worms), *mail logs* (containing data of completed and pending e-mail transactions, including sender and recipient address, subject, time stamp, and size), *Web server logs* (containing data on requests made to Web server and statistical information about network traffic; data may include source IP address of requesting host, confirmation and size of satisfied request, userid based on HTTP authentication), *application software logs* (activity related to use of particular software programs), *DHCP logs* (dynamic host configuration protocol data used to map a unique IP address to a device at a specific time), and so forth.

[3] The role of the IT expert witness will be discussed in the context of how his or her role in assisting the trier of fact to understand the evidence or to determine a fact in issue comports with current legal rules governing evidence admissibility, as well as how this role fulfills conjectured yet probable trends in the application of evidence law to digital artifacts.

[4] Hunter, P. (2002). W*orld Without Secrets*. New York: John Wiley & Sons.

[5] Lyman, P., and Varian, H. (2003). How much information? Available at http://www.sims.berkeley.edu/research/projects/how-much-info/how-much-info.pdf.

[6] *Webster's Revised Unabridged Dictionary*. Available at http://dictionary.reference.com/search?q=00-database-info&db=web1913.

[7] Mearian, L. (2003). Trades at top speed. *Computerworld,* 3 March. Available at http://www.computerworld.com/databasetopics/data/story/0,10801,78891,00.html

[8] See, e.g., Violino, B. Web services: waves of change. *Computerworld*, 19 May. Available at http://www.computerworld.com/softwaretopics/crm/story/0,10801,81251,00.html.

[9] Schwartz, M. (2001). Fraud busters: new technologies capable of handling secure, real-time transactions will help prevent, detect and prosecute B2B e-commerce fraud. *Computerworld*, 19 February. Available at http://www.computerworld.com/securitytopics/security/story/0,10801,57770,00.html.

[10] Id. (Noting a Gartner Group Inc. forecast that the worldwide business-to-business exchange market will grow to $7.29 trillion by 2004.)

[11] Id. (The average organization loses about 6% of its total annual revenue to fraud from customers and business partners and from abuses committed by its own employees, according to the Association of Certified Fraud Examiners in Austin, Texas. The association pegs the total fraud and abuse price tag for U.S. organizations at $400 billion annually.)

[12] Thornton, J. (1997). The general assumptions and rationale of forensic identification. In: *Modern Scientific Evidence: The Law and Science of Expert Testimony*, Vol. 2. St. Paul: West Publishing Co. (Forensic scientists have almost universally accepted the Locard Exchange Principle. This doctrine was enunciated early in the twentieth century by Edmund Locard, the director of the first crime laboratory, in Lyon, France. Locard's Exchange Principle states that with contact between two items, there will be an exchange. By recognizing, documenting, and examining the nature and extent of this evidentiary exchange, Locard observed that criminals could be associated with particular locations, items of evidence, and victims. The detection of the exchanged materials is interpreted to mean that the two objects were in contact.)

[13] Chmielewski, D. (2003). Online file-sharing networks bring porn into workplaces. *Mercury News*, 17 March. Available at http://www.siliconvalley.com/mld/siliconvalley/5413422.htm.

[14] See, e.g., Palisade Systems, Inc. (2003). Peer-to-peer study results: downloading porn tops peer-to-peer usage. Palisade Systems, Inc. Available at http://www.palisadesys.com/news&events/p2pstudy.pdf [cite case where woman claims sex harassment and court says no proof].

[15] See Kenneally, E. (2000). The byte stops here: liability for negligent computer security. *Computer Security Institute Annual Computer Security Journal*, Fall. Available at www.gocsi.com/byte.pdf; see generally, CERT/CC-Computer Emergency Response Team/Coordination Center, available at http://www.cert.org; Security Alert for Enterprise Resources, available at http://www.safermag.com; Security Focus, available at www.securityfocus.com; Bugtraq, available at www.bugtraq.securepoint.com; SANS Security Newsletters and Digests Services, available at http://www.sans.org/newsletters/; Microsoft Technical Updates, Microsoft Security Bulletins, available at http://www.microsoft.com/technet/security; VulnWatch, available at www.vulnwatch.com.

[16] Arms, W. (2000). *Digital Libraries*. Cambridge: MIT Press. Available at http://www.cs.cornell.edu/wya/DigLib/new/Chapter7.html.

[17] Schneier, B. (2000). *Secrets & Lies: Digital Security in a Networked World*, 1st ed. New York: John Wiley & Sons.

[18] *Lugashi*, 205 Cal.App.3d 632 (1988).

[19] *US v. Whitaker,* 127 F. 3d 602 (7th Cir. 1997).

[20] *US v. Glasser*, 773 F.2d 1559 (11th Cir. 1985).

[21] *US v. Bonallo*, 858 F.2d 1436 (9th Cir. 1998).

[22] See *United States v. Tank*, 200 F.3d 627 (9th Cir. 2000).

[23] See *Wisconsin v. Schroeder* 2000 WL 675942, citing *United States v. Catabran*, 836 F.2d 453, 458 (9th Cir. 1988) ("any question as to the accuracy of the printouts ...would have affected only the weight of the printouts, not their admissibility."). As for challenges to completeness, *Tank* referenced *United States v. Soulard* , 730 F.2d 1292, 1298 (9th Cir. 1984) ("once adequate foundational showings of authenticity and relevancy have been made, the issue of completeness then bears on the Government's burden of proof and is an issue for the jury to resolve.").

[24] *Lugashi*, 252 Cal.Rptr. 434, 440–43 (Cal.Ct.App. 1988).

[25] Id. at 440–43.

[26] Id. See also, *California v. Martinez*, 990 P.2d 563, 581 (2000) ([testimony on the] "acceptability, accuracy, maintenance, and reliability" of computer software is not required to admit computer records).

[27] *US v. Wilson*, 322 F.3d 353, (5th Cir. 2003) (finding that the district court clearly erred in holding that the Government proved that the electronic document was sent by a preponderance of the evidence).

[28] *Blackston v. United States*, Civil Action No. MJG-88–1454, United States District Court for the District of Maryland, 778 F. Supp. 244 (1991).

[29] A similar contention had been rejected by the district court in the case of *United States v. Berman*, 825 F.2d 1053, 1056–57 (6th Cir. 1987).

[30] *Blackston*, 778 F. Supp. 244 at 246.

[31] "One way to establish [authenticity] is to show the 'chain-of-custody.'" *United States v. Grant*, 967 F.2d 81, 83 (2nd Cir. 1992). "[T]he purpose of the chain-of-custody rule is to insure that the substance offered into evidence is in substantially the same condition as when it was seized." *United States v. Santiago*, 534 F.2d 768, 769 (7th Cir. 1976) [citing *United States v. Brown*, 482 F.2d 1226 (8th Cir. 1973)]. See generally, Sanett, S. Authenticity as a requirement of preserving digital data and records. Available at http://www.iassistdata.org/publications/iq/iq24/iqvol241sanett.pdf (discussing how authentication is the action or activities that demonstrate that something is authentic); Arms, W. (2000). *Digital Libraries*. Available at http://www.cs.cornell.edu/wya/DigLib/new/Chapter7.htm (discussing access management, authentication, and security).

[32] Vide infra, Part III Anatomy of Law Applied to Logs; see Peritz, supra, note 8 at 983–1003; see generally, Kerr, supra, note 97; Sommer, P. (1998). Intrusion detection systems as evidence. Presented at RAID 98': First International Workshop on the Recent Advances in Intrusion Detection. Available at http://www.raid-symposium.org/raid98/Prog_RAID98/Full_Papers/Sommer_text.pdf.

[33] Id. Sommer.

[34] See Fenner, supra, note 176 at 25 (quoting the late Irving Younger).

[35] See Peritz, supra, at 984–1002.

[36] This concept was discussed during a mock trial session lead by Professor Steven Cribari, University of Denver School of Law, ITRA Digital Evidence and Computer Forensics For Attorneys Conference, San Diego, CA (January 2003). Available at http://www.frallc.com/pdf/c110.pdf.

[37] See McElhaney, supra, note 122.

[38] See FED R. EVID. 803(6), supra, note 106.

[39] For example, some popular data-wiping software programs available include Evidence Eliminator, BCWipe, Eraser, SecureClean,East-Tec Eraser, and PGPWipe.

[40] 198.254.14.128 is the Internet Protocol (IP) address for a computer. Recognizing obvious differences, the IP is a numerical identifier for a host computer on the Internet, analogous to the address of a house in the physical world. See generally, DARPA Information Processing Techniques Office. (1981). Internet Protocol. Available at http://spectral.mscs.mu.edu/RFC/rfc0791.html.

[41] Peritz, supra, note 8 at 982.

[42] See Kenneally, E.E., and Swienton, Anjali. (2005). Presented at American Academy of Forensic Sciences Annual Conference, "Digital Evidence Mock Trial Workshop"; "Poking the Wookie Defenses in Digital Evidence Cases," New Orleans, LA; see generally, The Chewbacca defense, available at http://en.wikipedia.org/wiki/Chewbacca_Defense.

[43] FED. R. EVID. 702 and 703; Paoli R.R. Yard PCB Litigation, 53 F.3d at 747.

[44] *Taylor v. State*, 93 S.W.3d 487, 507 (Tex.App.Texarkana) (October 2002). (Here a law enforcement officer examined the defendant's hard drive and opined on the accuracy of the computer evidence copying procedure via testimony that he observed matching hash marks (i.e., the acquisition hash matched the verification hash and was concurrent with copying the computer evidence) on his computer screen at the time the copying process was completed. The officer made no manual recording of this in any form, although the forensic software used a verification process that would have provided written documentation of the quality of the copying procedure).

The initial question is whether information observed on a computer screen, generated not by a human source but setting out the results of a computer program in analyzing data, is hearsay .... Arguably, this should constitute such a statement. When the rules were written, computers were not capable of performing such analysis and at most would have provided raw data which would have to be analyzed by a human. Now, the computer program performs the analysis and a human only looks to see what result the program has reached.... Under this scenario, there is arguably a statement being made – just not by a human – but by an artificial intelligence.

Without going into the details of this type of analysis, however, as pointed out by the State, several courts of appeals have held that computer-generated information, whether on a display or paper, is simply not hearsay because it falls outside the strict language of the rule. This position is defensible and is apparently the sole position taken in Texas to date for materials not input into a computer and simply printed out, but that result from analysis done by the computer. The statement by Marshall was not hearsay.

Index

133